G000075035

A guide to

Promoting your Business

The ultimate workbook
for business owners

Antonia Chitty

This book is dedicated to David, without whom I wouldn't have got this far.

I also want to thank friends and clients who, despite being busy businesswomen and mums,
have taken the time to give me feedback, share resources and answer questions.
The book wouldn't have even existed without Kath and Anita's promptings.
In particular, thanks go to Amy, Anita, Bex, Della, Elaine, Lisa and Vicki for commenting on the draft.

Antonia Chitty, 18 Spencer Mews, London SW8 1HF
© Antonia Chitty 2007

Design and illustration www.greensanddesign.co.uk
Photography www.chrisperceval.co.uk
Printed by Cambrian Printers Limited, Aberystwyth
ISBN 9780955534508

Introduction

If you run your own business, you often have to become an instant expert in every area. Sometimes you can do this by yourself, other times it pays to get the professionals in.

With this book, you get the next best thing to having an expert working alongside you. I run my own business and have tried and tested the promotion techniques in this book on my enterprise. As a public relations professional, I have also advised hundreds of clients on how to promote their businesses.

This book has grown out of a series of fact sheets I wrote for clients who wanted to do their own PR. Since the fact sheets were first created, I have run training courses for clients ranging from childminders to creative arts students, and developed new material, all of which I have drawn upon for this handbook.

Do not just read this and then put it away. Read the examples, then get a pen, fill in the exercises, and make notes. This book will become a vital tool when promoting your business. You can find further resources to help you at www.prbasics.co.uk.

Spend 15 minutes a day doing one task to promote your business. Have this book on hand, refer to it to find out what you have planned, and how to go about it. Use what you have learnt every day to make a real difference to your business.

Best wishes for promoting your business.

Antonia Chitty

"This workbook is an excellent and concise guide to help anyone who is starting up a new business – it gives some excellent advice, guidance and knowledge for new business owners and entrepreneurs. When we started Organix, 15 years ago, tight funding meant we were almost totally dependent upon PR to build brand awareness. It was a crucial element to build the business and get across the passion and integrity that go into our foods for children. Today, PR remains an essential part of our business, and a key tool for reaching out to parents.

Lizzie Vann MBE, Founder of Organix Brands Ltd

Contents

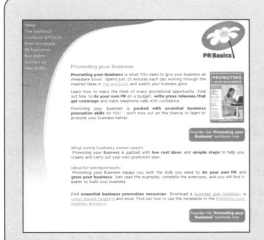

www.prbasics.co.uk

PR Basics offers resources to download to help you use this book.

Visit the site for hundreds of links and more help with business promotion.

Your website

Writing to promote your business

Special offers

Evaluating your progress

How have you done?

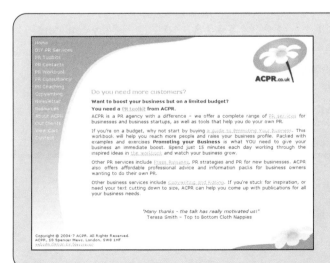

www.acpr.co.uk

ACPR can help you do your own PR.

You can buy databases of media contacts or get your press release written for you.

Where are you now?

Before you get stuck in, take a few moments to examine how you feel about promoting your business. Circle where you are now on each measure. We will look at this again when you have completed the book.

I feel confident about promoting my business:

Not at all confident   1 2 3 4 5 6 7 8 9 10   Very confident

I have clear objectives for my business:

No objectives   1 2 3 4 5 6 7 8 9 10   Well-defined objectives

I know who I am targeting with my promotion:

I'm very unsure   1 2 3 4 5 6 7 8 9 10   I know who I am targeting

I have clear plans for promoting my business:

No plans at all   1 2 3 4 5 6 7 8 9 10   Clear, well thought out plans

I am confident about writing a press release:

I'm very unsure   1 2 3 4 5 6 7 8 9 10   I can write a press release

I am confident about making telephone calls to promote my business:

Not at all confident   1 2 3 4 5 6 7 8 9 10   Very confident

I know about my local media and how to use it for promotion:

I know nothing about my local media   1 2 3 4 5 6 7 8 9 10   I know all about my local media

I am confident about promoting my business on the internet:

Not at all confident   1 2 3 4 5 6 7 8 9 10   Very confident

I am confident about writing to promote my business:

Not at all confident   1 2 3 4 5 6 7 8 9 10   Very confident

I know how to evaluate which promotions work well for my business:

I have no idea what works well   1 2 3 4 5 6 7 8 9 10   I am clear what works well

Getting started

It is not hard to learn how to promote your business better, but the key to success is to make it part of your daily routine. Just fifteen minutes a day or a single task will help to keep your business profile high. This guide is packed with simple ideas, many of which are low cost too. So, follow the ideas, plan in a daily promotional activity, and your business will grow.

Using this book

This is a workbook, so keep a pen with it, and make sure you write all over it! Each written section is accompanied by examples, so if you are not clear after reading the text, read the example to see how another business has done it. Try the exercises too — most of them can be done with just a pen and this workbook, although you may then need to go on and show what you have done to someone else for a second opinion, or write something up on your computer, if you use one. There are lots of online resources to help you which you can download from www.prbasics.co.uk.

Download this from www.prbasics.co.uk

Promotion — the basics

Here are a few basic promotion tips, so you can get started right away. First of all, make sure everyone knows what you do. Do not be embarrassed to talk about your work. Use your networks — old friends, family members, people you meet in a coffee shop or at the school gate — you never know who may be interested in your product or service. If someone asks you what you do, start by saying "I run my own business". Then, explain all about it. Prepare a 30 second sentence that sums up what you do — you never know who you may be speaking to. See the exercise at the end of this section for more help with this.

Always keep business cards in your pocket. This saves you searching for a pen and scrap of paper if someone shows an interest in your business. If you have single-sided business cards, use the back to write down something personal, related to what you were discussing. This will make it more likely that the recipient will retain the card. It could be extra contact details, a date, an event, or a product recommendation.

It is cheap and easy to run off sticky labels with your logo and web address on and to stick these on every letter you post — business or not.

What's my USP?

Now that you are thinking about how to tell people about your business, it is time to look at what you are saying to them. You may have a great business with lots to offer customers, but can you get your message across clearly and succinctly? A concise sentence or two summing up what your business offers is essential, for all your promotional materials as well as face-to-face situations.

Working out your 'Unique Selling Points' (USPs) will help you promote your business, and show everyone what is great about it. The example overleaf shows you how one business owner worked out how best to put her business across.

Jane's Toys
12 High Street, Fordfield
Bucks BU26 9RD

Tel: 01993 864 272
Fax: 01933 864 273
Email: info@janestoys.co.uk
www.janestoys.co.uk

Jane's Toys

Jane Porter
Manager

Unique Fair Trade Wooden and Traditional Toys

⏲ TWO MINUTE TIP

It is free to put your business name, web address and logo at the bottom of every email you send — and good advertising too. Think about other ways you can let people know about your business by simply using your logo, labels and business cards.

Example: USPs

Jane runs an online toy store, Jane's Toys. She has asked her friend to listen and make notes while she describes the business.

She says, "Well, we have lots of really nice stuff. There are traditional wooden things, you know, cars, trucks, and we've got some lovely dolls – not the plastic ones, rag dolls you can dress. We get them from a project in India, they supply lots of our stuff, and it is all fair trade. Lots of the things you can't get anywhere else – we're the only ones who sell them in the UK. And, um, what else? Well, we try to send things next day so people get them quickly even though we're online and they are buying by mail order – it is really important because lots of our customers buy presents at the last minute. We can even wrap things and sometimes send them direct to the birthday child."

Her friend's notes:
• Nice, wooden • Cars, trucks, dolls • India • Fair trade • Online/mail order • Next day • Presents • Gift service • Stuff you can't get elsewhere

Jane makes a list of the key words, drawn from the notes:
* *Wooden and traditional toys – covers the vehicles and dolls*
* *Fair Trade*
* *Unique – sums up "stuff you can't get elsewhere" in one word*
* *Next-day delivery and gift-wrap service.*

Using her key words, Jane comes up with a new phrase, which she will use on her website and business stationery, in her emails and advertising: Jane's Toys, Unique Fair Trade Wooden and Traditional Toys.

She will add, "Next-day delivery and gift-wrap service" underneath the main summary of her business where there is space on flyers and the website.

✐ EXERCISE: Your USPs

Now it is your turn. Try this simple exercise to help you pin down what stands out about your business.

Sit down with a friend, and spend five minutes telling them all about your business. Explain to them what you can offer and why they should get it from you. Ask them to make a note of the key things that stand out to them. If you do not have a willing victim to hand, just try talking out loud and jot down key words as you talk.

After you have finished talking, look at the words noted down. Turn these points and phrases into a few sentences, which sum up your business's good points.

Repeat the exercise with someone else, trying out your new phrases. It should take less time to get your key points across, and they should be clear about the benefits you can offer.

Now, break down the phrases that sum up your business even further. Highlight the key words and use them to devise a slogan.

⇨ **THINK ABOUT... Getting an advisor**
It is really helpful to have someone you can turn to for advice on setting up your business. Ask your local enterprise agency if they have any mentoring schemes, or start networking to find an experienced businessperson who you can bounce ideas off on a regular basis.

Your notes

Your notes

What is promotion?

You need to plan a range of activities to promote your business. In order to promote it effectively, you need to start thinking about it as early as possible.

Spreading the word

Many of the techniques in this workbook will help you spread the word about your goods or services. You may want to sell to customers directly, or need to work out how to attract them to your store, online or on the high street. Alternatively, you may be targeting retailers to purchase from you.

You will want to build relationships with customers and devise ways to encourage them to return and purchase again. Working through this handbook will help you develop lots of different ways to communicate with buyers.

Public relations and promotion

If you are looking for a product or service that you have not used before, a recommendation from a friend can help. Equally, an independent and objective mention in the press is just as useful (for example, I always like to read a restaurant review before choosing where to eat). Getting coverage for your business in a newspaper or magazine can beat splashing out on advertising, because journalists are not paid to run stories that feature your product or service. When they do cover your business, it carries the added weight of a third party opinion. If their opinion is positive, the impact on what people think about your business is invaluable. This is where public relations, or PR, is invaluable.

The Wikipedia definition of public relations is "the art of managing communication between an organisation and its key publics to build, manage and sustain a positive image". PR is all about using the media to raise your profile and generate positive publicity for your business. You may use a press release to inform the media about your business, but PR needs to go beyond that. Try to develop relationships with key people in your target media so that they are interested in you and your business, and you provide them with appropriate and newsworthy stories.

BUCKINGHAM CHRONICLE Monday 05 March 2007

Local businesswoman wins national award for initiative

Fordfield 'mumtrepreneur' Jane Porter has been recognised by a panel of experts for her successful business promotion skills

Jane, 36, who runs Jane's Toys, specialising in the sale of Fair Trade wooden and traditional toys, won the Promotion and PR category at the annual Small Business Council awards ceremony held at the Grosvenor Hotel in London last week.

The judges were unanimous in their decision to award the winning title to Jane's Toys for a recent mailing campaign which saw sales increase by over 45%. A profit of over £20,000 is predicted for the year. Speaking after the ceremony Jane said 'I am overjoyed to have been recognised, it has made all my hard work — and that of my staff — worthwhile.'

The panel of judges included key industry figures such as Terry Smart of SmartKids and Lord Hawkins, founder of Hawkins Toys as well as celebrity mums including actress Kate

Beyond the media, the skills you learn will help you communicate with staff and other stakeholders in the business, such as shareholders, suppliers, etc.

Good PR does not only bring customers to you; it can also make customers choose your business over someone else's. Public relations must be a planned and sustained effort. Think about the aims and objectives you have for your business. Plan your activities to publicise your business over a year. Monitor the coverage you get – and evaluate the amount of business it brings.

Think about how much time you want to spend on your business, and how much business you want to generate. A plug in a national paper or magazine could generate enquiries and keep you busy for days.

Be committed. Keep this book to hand, follow each action, and there is every opportunity for you to achieve more than you ever thought possible.

Smart objectives for smart promotion

When planning how to publicise your business, it is essential that you tie in your promotion objectives with your business objectives. Look at the aims and objectives in your business plan. If you do not have a business plan, then start to write one. There are plenty of templates online, (see www.prbasics.co.uk) or your local Business Link/Business Gateway can help.

Think about where you want the business to be in five years. What do you need to achieve to get there? How many items do you need to sell, what are your financial targets? If you are in business already, look at your past sales patterns. Have you been monitoring where customers hear about you? Have you measured the results of press coverage or advertising? (See the section on *Evaluating your business promotion* for more help with this). And what proportion of enquiries or visitors to your website turn into actual sales?

If you are just starting up, you will need to feel your way and adapt your promotion plans as you go along, but developing some firm ideas about where you want the business to go is a great start.

Your objectives should be clear and detailed enough for you to know exactly what you want to achieve. A useful acronym for developing objectives is SMART – meaning specific, measurable, achievable, realistic and timely.

SMART objectives

Specific – be clear about what you want to achieve.

Measurable – you should be able to measure whether you are meeting the objective.

Achievable – will you be able to actually do what you have planned?

Realistic – can you realistically meet the objectives with the resources you have?

Timely – include a timescale in which to meet the objective.

Example: Business objectives

Jane wants her business "to be making a profit in three years' time." It is a valid aim for the business but it does not give her much help in how to get to the desired profitable stage. First, let us break it down into some SMART objectives for Jane to build her plans on.

Jane already has various facts to hand that will help her develop her objectives. She can estimate how many sales she will need to make, how much profit she gets from her sales, and she has planned in what expenditure she will need to make over the next three years.

She could therefore develop an objective: "To be getting 20 orders a week by the end of this year, 30 by the end of year two, and 40 by the end of year three." She has included timescales, is specific about the number of orders she wants, and can measure how the business is performing. However, she also needs to look at whether this is achievable and realistic. What promotion will she need to do to reach these targets? And is this objective the only thing she needs?

As well as just looking at the number of orders she needs to achieve, Jane could make

Jane could make her business more profitable by increasing the value of orders, and increasing repeat orders from existing customers.

her business more profitable by increasing the value of orders, and increasing repeat orders from existing customers. She might want to attract new customers, increase the number of visitors to her website, and get people signed up for a newsletter. So, Jane's initial objective, "To be getting 20 orders a week by the end of this year, 30 by the end of year two, and 40 by the end of year three" breaks down into the following more detailed objectives:

"In order to make my business turn a profit within three years I plan to:

- *Increase my weekly orders from 20 in year one to 27 in year two and 35 in year three.*
- *Increase the average amount spent on each order from £15 in year one, to £20 in year two and £25 in year three.*
- *Increase the number of items in each purchase from one to two in year one.*
- *Increase the number of visitors to my website from 50 a day in year one, to 100 a day in year two, and 200 a day in year three.*
- *Attract subscribers to a newsletter, aiming for 500 in year one, 1000 in year two and 3000 in year three."*

Next, Jane needs to look at her resources and see what she might be able to do to achieve her plans. This more detailed planning will feed into her promotion plan, and she may need to modify her objectives as she determines whether or not they are realistic.

Jane has drawn up a list of actions as follows:
- *To ensure that everyone who buys from her website spends a little bit more, she is planning to promote 'add-on' items at the check out stage. As cards and wrapping paper are often needed for gifts, she may offer those. She also will develop a range of*

toys costing a few pounds, which could be added in as a last minute extra.
- *She will offer free postage for orders over her target figures of £15 in year one, £20 in year two, and £25 in year three.*
- *She will write a press release about the new items available and the free postage, and also mention them in her newsletter.*
- *She is also going to review the publications she advertises in, aiming more at people with higher incomes, to help increase average spend. She will request a 'media pack' from potential publications which will provide her with information about who reads the magazine, how many copies it sells, and the standard costs of advertising (for more on this, see the Advertising section on page 32).*
- *In order to get more people to subscribe to her newsletter, she will offer discounts to subscribers, and ask them to pass the newsletter on to friends. She is also making plans to link up with various websites which are read by her target audience, and attract more visitors through offers and promotions exclusive to those sites.*

By working through these ideas, and seeing if she has the time to do the activities and the finances to pay for the promotion, Jane can make sure that she can actually achieve her plans.

⏱ TWO MINUTE TIP

Look at Jane's objectives and actions and highlight which ones might be relevant to your business too.

✎ **EXERCISE:**
Now fill in your SMART objectives

Start noting down ideas for activities you might do to meet the objectives – we will look at making them into a detailed plan on page 22.

1

2

3

4

5

Before you move on, remember that your objectives are not set in stone. You may need to adapt them as time passes. If your business grows faster than you planned, you may have met your year one objectives after six months. Or, if it does not look like you are going to meet an objective, look at the activities you are doing to get there, and alter or increase them. Review all your objectives at the end of each year and see if the objectives for the next year are still realistic and achievable. If not, then rewrite them accordingly.

Find your target audience

When you are working out your plans for promotion, it helps if you have a clear idea about who you are trying to reach.

If you have an existing business, think about your current customers and those who you would like to attract to purchase from your business. If you are just starting up, you may need to use a bit of imagination to work out who your potential customers are, but with a little market research you can find out a lot of information.

> ⇨ **THINK ABOUT...**
> ## The benefits of market research
> Remember that a little research now can save you hundreds or thousands of pounds in the long run. Test your market before you invest money in your business, and you will know how to best target your funds.

Using a survey

Whether you are in business already or just at the planning stages, a survey is a useful tool to help you pin down the right groups of people to aim your promotion activities at. You can ask people about your products or services and get feedback on whether they might buy, and if not, why not. The example opposite, will give you plenty of ideas about what you should include, and it can be easily customised to cover your business area.

It is important to look at the demographics – where people live, what age they are, what their income is, whether they own a home, etc. You will also want to include a section asking about your products or services and pricing. You may also want

---

⌐◉ USEFUL RESOURCES: Enterprise organisations

For help with business planning

- Business Link, England:
  www.businesslink.gov.uk, 0845 6009006
- Business Eye, Wales:
  www.businesseye.org.uk, 08457 969798
- Venture Wales:
  www.venturewales.com, 0845 0453150
- Welsh Assembly Government:
  new.wales.gov.uk/topics/businessandeconomy
- Highlands and Islands Enterprise, Scotland:
  www.hie.co.uk, 01463 234171
- Business Gateway, Scotland:
  www.bgateway.com
- Scottish Enterprise:
  www.scottish-enterprise.com, 0845 6078787
  (from within Scotland) or 0141 228 2000
  (from anywhere in the UK)

- Scottish Development International:
  www.scotent.co.uk, 0141 228 2828
- Invest Northern Ireland:
  www.investni.com, 028 9023 9090

Write in more resources you discover:

_____

_____

_____

_____

_____

> ⇒ **THINK ABOUT... The size of your survey**
> Do not take on more than you can handle. It is better to do a small survey and be able to analyse the results than have hundreds of responses sitting in a box for months until you have time to look at them. If you can get 100 responses, that's great, but if not, make the most of the responses you do have.

to look at how the business is delivered, asking about people's preference for ways to pay, how to buy or order, etc. If you are planning advertising or press releases, find out about the papers and magazines they read.

Trial the questions on a few friends. You will need to be careful how you word the questions, and a trial run can ensure that everything is clear. You may want to offer a voucher or discount as an incentive to participate.

You may want to run an online survey, or a paper version. An online survey has many advantages, as with modern software it is easy to collate responses, and there is no need to laboriously copy out the answers. However, think about how appropriate an online survey is to the people you want views from. Will they be happy to use a PC? Are there any groups of people you won't be reaching this way? If, for example, you have an online store, an online survey may seem like a great idea. However, would you be missing out on a range of potential customers who might like your goods but are novices on the PC? You may decide to offer a paper version of the survey too.

Example: Surveys

Jane is testing out some of the new ideas she has for her business. She is sending the survey out with every order, and is also distributing it to some local playgroups and schools, with a 10% discount voucher for everyone who returns it. Here is a selection of her questions:

Are you:
1 Female
2 Male

Are you:
1 Single
2 Married
3 Living with partner
4 Divorced/separated

Are you:
1 Working full-time
2 Working part-time
3 In education/studying
4 Unemployed
5 Housewife/ house husband

What is your family income?
1 Under £4,000
2 £4,001 - £10,000
3 £10,001 - £20,000
4 £20,001 - £30,000
5 £30,001 - £40,000
6 £40,000 plus

If you have not bought from Jane's Toys before, would you be interested in buying Fair Trade Wooden and Traditional Toys?
1 Yes
2 No
3 I am an existing customer

Who would you buy for?
Tick all that apply
1 My own children
2 Nephews and/or nieces
3 Grandchildren
4 Friends' children
5 My children's school friends
6 Other – please fill in

_____

How much would you spend on a gift for a child?
1 Up to £5
2 £5 - £9.99
3 £10 - £14.99
4 £15 - £19.99
5 £20 - £24.99
6 £25 - £29.99
7 £30 - £34.99
8 £35+

Where would you prefer to make your purchase?
1 In a high street store
2 By mail order – postal
3 Through an online store
4 At a craft fair
5 Other – please fill in

_____

Would you use a gift-wrap service if buying online or by mail order?

1 Yes
2 No

How much would you be prepared to pay for gift-wrapping?

1 Up to £1
2 £1 - £1.99
3 £2 - £2.99
4 £3 - £3.99
5 £4 +

If you were buying a gift for someone else, would you add in a 'pocket money' toy as a treat for your own child?

1 Yes
2 No

How much would you be prepared to pay for a pocket money toy?

1 Up to £1
2 £1 - £1.99
3 £2 - £2.99
4 £3 - £3.99
5 £4 +

Which of the following national parenting magazines do you read?

1 Baby and Toddler Gear
2 Green Parent
3 I'm Pregnant
4 Junior
5 Junior Pregnancy and Baby
6 My Child
7 Mother and Baby
8 NewGen – NCT members magazine
9 Practical Parenting
10 Prima Baby
11 Pregnancy and Birth
12 Pregnancy, Baby and You
13 Other – please fill in

_____
_____
_____
_____

What other publications do you read?

1 Local newspaper
2 National daily newspaper
3 National weekend newspaper
4 Other – please fill in

_____
_____
_____
_____

✏ EXERCISE:
Do you need a survey?

Now, think about whether you want to do a survey. There are other options – you could get a group of about eight existing or potential customers together and spend an hour chatting through a prepared list of topics. This is called a 'focus group'. Ideally you would record the session, and then go back and listen to what people say. It should help you draw out in depth thoughts on your business. Or, you could come up with a list of questions and interview people on a one-to-one basis. Questions for this sort of interview do not necessarily need to be as formal as for a paper or online survey. One-to-one interviews can be good if you want to discuss sensitive topics such as finances or health.

Take some time to think about what you need to know to improve your business. If you are planning marketing and promotion, do you know enough about the people you want to reach?

Write down a selection of the things you need to find out here:

_____
_____
_____
_____
_____

Now think about the best way to find out the answers you need:

• Survey of a large group of people – ideal for finding out general views on a wide range of issues.
• Focus group with around eight people – ideal for getting more in depth and discussing the pros and cons of a few ideas.
• Semi-structured interviews – a series of one-to-ones which help you discuss issues in depth.

⇨ **THINK ABOUT...**
Analysing the comments

When analysing comments people have made, you may decide that it is too time consuming to type in every comment. Instead, decide to read them through when you have a few hours spare. Look at the responses to each section and note down new ideas or useful suggestions.

For promotional and advertising purposes, use your results to decide which publications will reach the sort of people who buy from your business. If you are aspiring to expand your business, think about the kind of people you want to reach too. Draw up a picture of them, think about their lifestyle, and this will help you work out how to promote your business to them.

Example:

Jane has drawn a stick figure and added notes to give her an idea of who she is targeting.

woman, age: 25-55
Has kids. Likes tv, magazines, local radio

Now draw the people you want your business to target. Use information from existing customers, or imagine the people you are reaching out to. What are they wearing, what are they saying?

It is easiest to analyse a survey if you give people a selection of boxes to tick. That way you can easily count up the number of replies. However, it is also good to leave some spaces for the respondents' own suggestions, which you can read through for inspiration. Plan how you will analyse the survey as you set it up. If you are familiar with Excel or similar database programs, set up a column for each question, and then enter each respondent's replies, one respondent per row. It is easiest if you use a 1 to represent a 'yes' and a 0 to represent a 'no' response. You can then use the 'sum' functions to add up the number of 'yes' and 'no' replies. For questions with multiple responses, set up one column per option, and simply enter a 1 in the column corresponding to the selected option. You can download a template from www.prbasics.co.uk.

Download this from www.prbasics.co.uk

⌐◑ **USEFUL RESOURCES:**
Surveys

Create an online survey at info.zoomerang.com or www.surveymonkey.com. Both have free options, and Survey Monkey lists 33 other online survey providers on its 'pricing' page if you want to shop around for more paid features.

Write in more resources you discover:

_____

_____

_____

_____

Making your promotion plan

Public relations should never be a one-off effort. To be effective, PR needs to become part of your daily routine. So far, we have thought about your aims and objectives, and you have read a little about how promotional activities can help you to achieve them.

In this section, we will look at creating a promotional plan for your business, setting out your promotional activities for the next 6-12 months. This will keep your profile high, and make sure that potential customers always have your name at their fingertips.

Once you have drafted a plan for the first six months or year, keep on adding ideas as they come to you.

Start by making yourself a calendar or mini year planner. There is a blank planner included on page 26. However, once you get going you may need more space than this and it is simple to set something up on a computer. Create a table with up to five columns, and thirteen rows, including the header. (See opposite for an example or download a ready made template from www.prbasics.co.uk.)

Download this from www.prbasics.co.uk

✏ EXERCISE: Your promotion plan

Before you start to plan how you will promote your business, let us recap what you need to know. Fill in your answers in the space below, and keep them in mind when planning every activity.

What is unique and special about my business?

_____

_____

_____

_____

_____

What are my business objectives for the next 3-5 years?

_____

_____

_____

_____

_____

Who do I want to target with my promotions?

_____

_____

_____

_____

Month	Events	Activities	Targets	Promotional Tactics	Target Media	Evaluation
April	Real Nappy week	Stall at local NCT fair for parents to sign up for info	Local parents	Posters, leaflets, press release	Local paper	
May	New colour range available	Competition to win new colour product	Parents, existing website customers	Press release, Newsletter to existing customers	Parenting magazines and websites	

The months of the year go in the first column. The second column is titled 'Events'. Go through writing in seasonal dates and events that are relevant to your business. This could include promotional events, such as Real Nappy Week, or dates such as Valentines Day, Mothers Day, Easter, Christmas, and Back to School time. Then, have a look at your business plans, and see what events you have coming up. Still in column two, you should note down when you are planning to launch a new product or service online, or when you have a sale planned, etc.

In the third column, start jotting down activities you could tie in with the events. Think about holding a stall somewhere, running a promotion or a competition. You will also need to plan in regular monthly activities, such as networking, advertising, visiting certain websites. See page 24 for further ideas.

Column four is for your 'Targets'. Here, you should write down the target audience for each promotional activity. If you are holding a stall at a fair, the targets may be local residents. If it is a competition on your website, you will want to contact existing customers to draw them back to your site, and also highlight the competition to

> ⏱ **TWO MINUTE TIP**
> This may seem daunting at first — you might think, "How can I come up with a different promotional idea each month?" but working through the exercises in this book will help you break the task down into manageable chunks.

> ⏱ **TWO MINUTE TIP**
> While you are making your plan, refer back to your business objectives and check that each activity represents a small step towards achieving your targets.

other people who might be interested. Look at your previous work on target audiences and make sure that you have each group covered.

Column five is for 'Promotional Tactics', which can range from flyers and posters, to press releases and adverts. For each event or activity, think about whether you will need to issue a press release to let relevant magazines, papers and websites know what you are up to. If so, write down 'press release' in column five next to each relevant activity. (See the next chapter for detailed information on creating and sending a press release). Also use this column to write down when you plan to use leaflets and posters.

Use column six to note down which media you will be targeting. You will also need a seventh column for how you will evaluate the promotion. Leave it blank for the moment – or skip ahead to page 81 if you want to read about it now.

Timing

Now for the tricky bit – making sure that you do the right activity at the right time. If, for example, you are keen to get people to buy your product as a Christmas gift, you will need to start early – promotional activities in October or November will have more time to take effect, and you will catch

> ✏️ **EXERCISE: Creating your promotion plan**
>
> Look at the plan again, and start by pencilling in everything you have planned for your business. If you have blank months, do not worry. There may be other times that you have lots of promotional activities going on. Why not alter the timing so you have an even spread of events throughout the year. Or can you come up with something to fill the gap? How about developing a special promotional range for Halloween, for example. Or offer free postage during August, if you find that it is usually a quiet time for orders. Have a look on the internet for other promotional weeks that you could link into (see *Useful resources* on page 39). If you know when you will be on holiday, note that down too.

organised people who do their shopping in advance. Monthly magazines work approximately three months in advance, so you will need to send press releases for Christmas features in July.

Having come up with a draft plan, get your diary out. Go through each row, and work out what you will need to do when. Start by noting down three or four months in advance to send out press releases to monthly magazines. Pick a date a month to six weeks ahead to contact weekly magazines, and just a couple of weeks ahead for newspapers and websites. If you are going to need posters and leaflets, allow enough time to write them, and get them printed. By doing this it will become evident when you have too much to do, and, again, you can adjust your activities accordingly.

If you are full of ideas now, skip to page 26 and start filling in your plan.

> ⇒ **THINK ABOUT...**
> **Ongoing promotion planning**
> You do not have to complete your plan right now. The rest of this book is packed with ideas which you can add to your plan as you work through the exercises.

> 🕐 **TWO MINUTE TIP**
> Plan in regular email newsletters for existing customers and anyone who signs up on your website.

Help – I do not have enough ideas

Have a look at the following and see if you can adapt any of these ideas to use in your own promotion plans.

Leaflets

Draw up a target list for places to distribute your leaflets – stroll around places to see where your target audience hang out. As an example, depending on who you want to contact you could leave leaflets in coffee shops, business centres, toddler groups. Visit a new location each week, and remember to go back to places and see if you need to restock.

Displays and demonstrations

Do you have a topic you could talk about or a skill to show off? Would your business make an interesting subject for a talk? Think about Women's Institute Groups, Rotarians, local kids clubs, etc. Get a list of names and phone numbers and make some calls to find out how they book speakers, and what they like to hear about. Then see if you can plan a talk or demo that would be of interest.

Newsletters

Plan your newsletters for the year. Use a program such as Constant Contact (www.constantcontact .com) to send out a regular update on what you are

Public relations should never be a one-off effort. To be effective, PR needs to become part of your daily routine.

up to. Aim at sending out something bi-monthly or every month to let people know about special offers, updates and events.

Articles

Write some tips or an article. If you have some spare time use your expertise to write some top ten tips. Send this out to relevant publications and websites. See page 66 for more information on writing to promote your business.

Weblinks

Browse the internet to work out which websites are read by your target audience. See if you can submit your link to the relevant websites, or join and post on their forums.

Local papers

Buy your local paper and have a look at what they cover. See if you can plan in some activities which will be of interest to them, and of course, remember to send them press releases about what you have planned.

Be a case study

Find websites where journalists place media requests – many journalists advertise when they need case studies and you might be able to get some good coverage for you and your business by volunteering. Search on 'media requests' on the internet, and check out chat forums.

Local networking

Attend networking events. Enquire about your local business groups, Chamber of Commerce, etc and get to know other local businesses. Your local enterprise organisation may be able to help you find local groups.

Network online

There are many online business directories and forums. Subscribe for useful email newsletters, the opportunity to list your business in their directory and to 'chat' with other business owners and share and solve problems.

Online promotion

Look at the Adwords programmes offered by Google and other search engines and directories. You create a small text advert which appears when people use certain search terms. Swap website links and promotional materials with complementary businesses. (See *Promoting your business on the net,* page 59 for more information on this topic).

Events

Plan an event and press release to celebrate your business's anniversary.

Incentives

Develop incentives for customers to hand out your promotional materials and encourage their friends to buy from you.

Competitions

Enter competitions for your business such as start up awards. Search on the internet or ask your local enterprise centre if they know of any awards.

> ⇒ **THINK ABOUT...**
> **One step at a time**
> Do not be daunted by the plan you have before you. Set aside just 15 minutes each day for a promotional task, and you will soon find that you are successfully promoting your business.

Month	Events	Activities	Targets
April	Easter		
May	May Bank Holidays		
June	Fathers Day		
July	End of Term/ Summer Holidays		
August	Summer Holidays		
September	Back to School		
October	Halloween		
November	Fireworks Night		
December	Christmas		
January	New Year		
February	Valentines Day		
March	Mothers Day		

Other ideas:

Promotion	Target Media	Evaluation

Other ideas:

Your notes

Your notes

Promotional materials

This section will help you work out what materials you need to promote your business.

If you want to spread the word about your business, you will need some materials to help. Look at your promotion plan. Have you planned to distribute postcards or flyers or posters? Do you have business cards to hand out at networking events? Will potential customers want a catalogue or brochure? And what about letterheads or compliments slips? (We will look at online promotion later in the workbook, see page 56 onwards.)

Creating a logo

First, think about your logo. You can simply sketch out your own ideas and ask a designer to convert them into an electronic format, or pay for someone to create something for you. Think about images which convey the key points you identified about your business. Try out a few different versions on people you know before you commit to a final choice.

Choosing a printer

Once you have a logo and a strapline, you can go ahead and produce the stationery you require. It is worth checking out local printers and looking at big online stores like www.vistaprint.co.uk. Be aware of the differences in print output terms when sending images or information to be printed. Some printers will specify how they wish to receive your information. And a document on screen may look different to the printed version. Ask the printer for a draft example if you can before he or she runs off a large quantity.

Specifications for print

CMYK (**C**yan, **M**agenta **Y**ellow Blac**K**) describes the image in terms of the amount of colour to be added to a white page to print, whereas on screen it is described as RGB – which indicates the amount of red, green and blue to be subtracted from black. You can save a document or image accordingly.

A JPEG is usually suitable for printing purposes, but be careful as repeated re-saving/resizing can lead to poor quality images particularly if you are printing something large. This is due to the compression the file format uses.

⌐🖰① USEFUL RESOURCES: Online printers

You may want to check out your local printer – the advantage of being able to collect your materials will save you time and delivery charges. However, look online to get a good idea of prices. Online print stores allow you to order whenever suits you too.

Online printers:

- www.promoprintstore.com
- www.robrook.com/price.htm
- www.solopress.com/index.php
- www.vistaprint.co.uk

Add in more printers:

⇨ THINK ABOUT...
Making the most of the space

Are you making the most of your space?
Do you want to print on both sides of each
item? Business cards can be printed both
sides, or you may want to add stickers each
month to advertise your current promotion.
If you do not print on the back, make sure
you add a little personal note when handing
them out (see page 9).

A TIFF is the preferred format to ensure a good
quality image but as these do not use compression
they can be quite big and are not always suitable
for emailing. For web images a JPEG or GIF is
usually fine. See the section on *Advertising* for
further details on image size and resolution.

How many copies of each?

It is often cheaper to buy large quantities, an
additional thousand may only cost a fraction of the
first thousand, but make sure you have plans for
distributing each and every flyer or you will just have
an expensive pile of waste paper. Add up how many
copies of each item you will leave in places, swap
with other businesses, and send to customers. You
may want to add 10 per cent to allow for extras,
but think carefully before you go further. Are you
including pricing information? How long will this
remain current? If you are printing glossy
catalogues that you hope will have a long life, it may
be more cost-effective to do a separate price list on
plain paper to allow you to update prices at will.

✎ EXERCISE:
Promotional materials action plan

What stationery do I need?
Posters • Postcards • Business cards
Compliments slips • Letter-headed paper
Other – your suggestions

_____

_____

Get quotes from a couple of printers. Ask for
the price for 100 copies, 500 copies and
1000 copies, for example. Check delivery
charges too.

Printer 1:

_____

Printer 2:

_____

Printer 3:

_____

Fill in the details:

_____

_____

Jane's Toys
12 High Street, Fordfield
Bucks BU26 9RD

Tel: 01993 864 272
Fax: 01933 864 273
Email: info@janestoys.co.uk
www.janestoys.co.uk

With compliments

Unique Fair Trade Wooden and Traditional Toys

Jane's Toys
12 High Street, Fordfield
Bucks BU26 9RD

Tel: 01993 864 272
Fax: 01933 864 273
Email: info@janestoys.co.uk
www.janestoys.co.uk

Jane Porter
Manager

Unique Fair Trade Wooden and Traditional Toys

**Jane's Toys business card ↑
← and compliments slip**

Advertising

It is easy to overspend on advertising, and hard to predict how well it will work for you. A little careful preparation will ensure that you make the most of your advertising budget, however small.

Decide an approximate annual budget for advertising. To do this, request some media packs from magazines and newspapers that you might like to advertise in. In a media pack, the rate card will show you the standard rate for advertisement. You should aim to negotiate a discount of up to 50 per cent on this rate. Work out where you would like to advertise, add it up, and then revise your list of targets to meet what you can afford.

When planning advertising, ask yourself whether your target audience will read your advert? If you are a high street business and want local customers, do not be tempted by advertising in national publications if a local publication will reach your potential customers at a fraction of the cost. Look at the magazine or paper yourself and see where your advert would fit in. Will it stand out, or will it be lost amongst thousands of others?

Once you have made your list of targets, check out deadlines and get an advert drawn up. If you have an advert all ready, you will be able to take advantage of last minute rates. Try to include a striking image and memorable logo. Make sure the advertisement highlights your business's unique and special points. Check that the advert will look good in black and white and colour – you may want different versions and a range of sizes. The media packs will tell you what format different publications require. As a general guideline a PDF or JPEG will be acceptable, and the higher the resolution the better. Aim for a minimum of 300dpi (dots per inch).

Negotiating the best price

Once you have your advert drawn up, call shortly before the deadline and see if there is any space available. Do not sound too keen, and ask what would be the 'best price'. If you don't get the price you want, you can play it cool. Say that you will think about it, once they have your contact details, and see if they call you back with a better offer. Of course, this strategy means that you risk missing the slot, but there is always next month's issue.

✎ EXERCISE:
Target your advertising

Fill in your target publications for advertising. Some you will have in mind already, but why not go and browse in a big newsagents for other similar publications, or look on the internet.

1 _____

2 _____

3 _____

4 _____

5 _____

6 _____

7 _____

8 _____

9 _____

10 _____

Advertising checklist

When booking an advert, ask yourself the following questions:

- Will this reach the right target audience?
- Have I asked for a discount on the standard rate?
- Is it on my list of target publications?
- Could I reach the same target audience for less expenditure?

⏱ TWO MINUTE TIP

If a sales person approaches you for advertising do not be persuaded unless they are on your list of targets. You can always think about including their publication for advertising later on, if they really are right for your business.

Unique Fair Trade Wooden and Traditional Toys

- **Wide range of traditional toys including cars, trains, rag dolls, jigsaw puzzles and much more**
- **Products sourced from Fair Trade suppliers**
- **Next-day delivery and free gift-wrapping**

Jane's Toys, 12 High Street, Fordfield, Bucks BU26 9RD
Tel: 01993 864 272 • Fax: 01933 864 273 • Email: info@janestoys.co.uk

↑ **Example of a magazine advert for Jane's Toys**

RNIB clear print guidelines

Make sure everyone can read your materials. Follow these guidelines and everyone will find them clear. The solutions are straightforward and inexpensive, focusing on some basic design elements, including font, type size, and contrast.

Type size: Use between 12 and 14 point. The larger the minimum type size, the more people you will reach.

Contrast: Better contrast between the background and the text makes the text more legible. Contrast is affected by the size and weight of the type. Black text on a white background provides the best contrast. If using white type, make sure the background colour is dark enough to provide sufficient contrast.

Typeface: Avoid highly stylised typefaces, such as those with ornamental, decorative or hand-written styles.

Type styles: Lots of capital letters, underlined or italicised text are harder to read.

Leading: The space between one line of type and the next (known as leading) is important. Aim for 1.5 to 2 times the space between words on a line.

Type weight: People with sight problems often prefer bold or semi-bold weights to normal ones. Avoid light type weights.

Word spacing and alignment: Keep to the same amount of space between each word. Do not condense or stretch lines of type. Align text to the left margin as it is easy to find the start of the next line and keeps the spaces even between words. Avoid justified text as uneven word spacing makes reading difficult.

Printing: Avoid glossy paper because glare makes it difficult to read, and choose uncoated paper that weighs over 90gsm.

Advice is taken from *See it Right: Making information accessible for people with sight problems (2006)*, Royal National Institute of the Blind, London. RNIB's clear print guidelines are based on experience of the issues over many years, advice from experts in the field and evidence including research into fonts and type size.

Writing a press release

A press release is a newsworthy story about your business that you submit to newspapers, radio, television or magazines. If the media is interested in your story, your press release may make it into in their publication.

You need to make sure that there is a story that will grab people's attention, so only issue a press release when you have something interesting to say. All releases need a 'hook' or 'angle', something that will appeal to editors and give your story a good chance of gaining coverage. Journalists are always on the look out for stories that will interest the readers of their paper or magazine.

Press releases follow a standard format. This makes it easy for the journalist to see what the story is about at a glance. It also means that, once you have a template to follow, it is simple for you to fill in your story too.

The first sentence of the press release needs to instantly capture the journalist's attention, and sum up the story. Focus on a problem you are solving for readers, and make sure you have a brief but attention-grabbing headline. Use the first paragraph to answer all the important questions like who, what, where, when, why and how. Get vital information in first, so if the journalist stops reading after the first paragraph, he or she has a good idea of the story. Then, back up your claims with facts and statistics in the following paragraphs.

Press releases – dos and don'ts

Use facts, and cut back on adjectives. Always use the present tense or the release can sound like old news, and write in the third person (he or she, instead of I). Include short quotes, in italics, highlighting new information that is not mentioned elsewhere in the press release. Write in the style of the magazine you are targeting as editors may just take your words and put them straight on the page.

If you are targeting different media sectors with the same story, write multiple releases rather than issuing one 'catch all' release.

Keep press releases to one or two sides of A4, double-spaced to give the editor room to scribble. Double spacing is less critical, however, if you are emailing a release. Use a clear modern font like Ariel, at least 10pt in size. Make paragraphs short for easy reading and align the text to the left. If you are sending your release by post, use A4 letterhead paper, and number your pages 1 of 2, 2 of 2, etc. Use only one side of the paper. If your release is more than one page, write 'more' at the bottom. Finish the press release with ### ENDS ###.

Make sure you include 'Notes to Editors'. This should include your phone number, address, company name, fax number, email and website. Include the hours you are available at the listed phone number and add an after hours phone number, if you can. You should also state whether you have photos available. See page 36 for a press release template or download one from www.prbasics.co.uk.

✏️ EXERCISE: News or not?

Now you know what a press release should look like, do not just get stuck in to writing straightaway. First of all, you need to think carefully about the content. Although everything about your business may seem interesting to you, editors and journalists receive hundreds of press releases each day, and you need to make sure that what you send in is newsworthy, appropriate to the publication, and stands out from the hundreds of other releases that arrive on a journalist's desk on a daily basis.

Buy your local papers and have a look at the sort of story they cover. Look at where businesses have made the headlines. What sort of story is it? Start cutting out items of interest. Now, think about what your target audience might read. Again, go through the publication and tear out relevant and appropriate stories. Repeat this with trade press, business and professional journals. When you have three piles of cuttings, go through each one and ask yourself the questions below. Jot down your answers and see if you come up with any trends, or just think about the stories you have looked at and review your ideas for press releases, bearing in mind what you have seen in the clippings you have made.

What is the main point of the story?	Who does the story interest?	What makes the story worth covering?	Who has written the story?

🕑 TWO MINUTE TIP

During your research, it is also useful to note down who wrote each story, as they may be a good target for your next press release. Do not throw out the newspapers; you may need to collect contact details from them later.

Your Logo

Press Release

Issued Date _____ For Immediate Release

OR Embargoed Until Date _____

Title... make it brief and attention-grabbing

The first sentence should be a summary of the story. Get your key points across to catch the journalist's attention or they may not read further. Answer all the important questions like who, what, where, when, why and how. Write as if you are speaking to the readers of the publication – review your target publication for an appropriate style.

Expand on the details in the second paragraph. Remember the journalist will want to know what is unique or new about your story and why it will appeal to their readers. Then, back up your claims with facts and statistics in the following paragraphs. Write in the present tense, and use 'he' or 'she' instead of 'I'.

Go on to illustrate your story with quotes, *"A quote, written in italics, from a key person, helps bring a story to life. Make sure your quote adds new information to the release".*

As well as quotes, you could use bullet points to highlight points about your story:

• Special
• Timely
• Unique

Finish off with details such as dates, times, how to order or contact you – this only needs to be brief, and should be the details you would like to see in print. Fuller details can go in 'Notes to Editors', opposite.

It's simple to add a photo or illustration to catch the journalist's eye and bring the press release to life. If you are emailing it, make sure you use a low resolution image, so the file isn't too large.

##Ends##

More/over

Page 1 of 2

↑ **Press release template**

Notes to Editors

1 Tell the editor who to contact for more information – include mobile, landline and email if possible.

2 Also include short background information on your company, when it was launched, achievements, mini biography of the founder, etc.

3 Include company name, fax number, email and website address.

4 Include opening hours, prices, venues, dates as appropriate to your story.

5 You should also state whether you have photos available.

Page 2 of 2

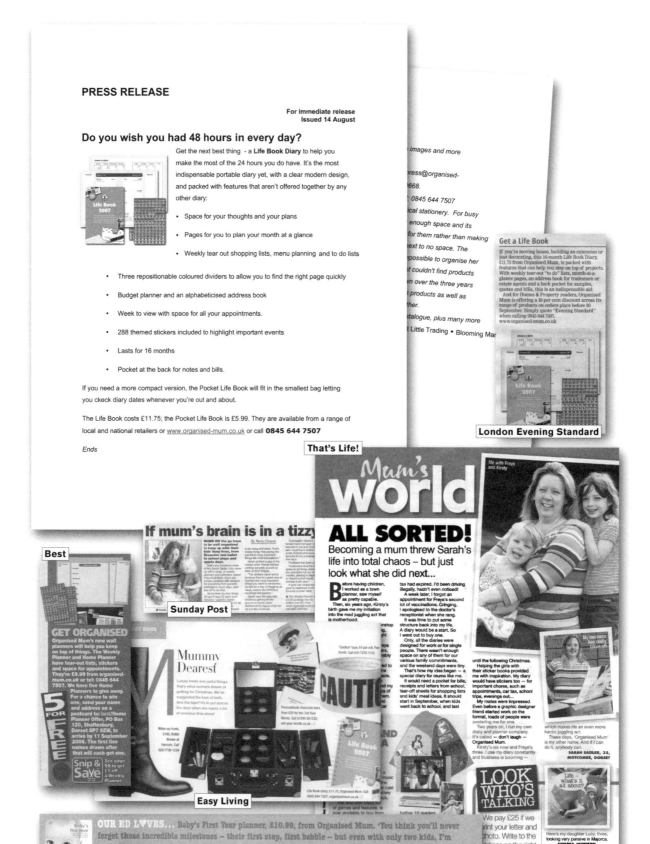

↑ **Real-life press release and coverage examples, Organised Mum**

Help – I need ideas for my press releases

Here is a selection of ideas to get you thinking. If this sparks off some ideas of your own, there is space at the bottom for you to add more ideas.

Business launch

Launch of your business, or business expansion – of interest to local papers and trade and business publications. You could also mention the launch of a new or updated website.

New products

New services or products: focus on the benefits to your customers and the publication's readers.

New staff

If you employ a new member of staff, let the local papers know. Highlight their specialist skills or the employment you are bringing to the area.

Achievements

Issue a press release when you or your employees are recognised for outstanding achievements or gain qualifications. Focus the release on how the award or qualification will help customers or clients.

People stories

Local and trade press often cover people stories, and both would be interested if celebrities or public figures use your services. Can you use contacts to get a celebrity to launch an event? If you have an interesting hobby this might interest local papers.

Unusual stories

Have you supplied something unusual or managed a rush delivery? Another one for local or trade press.

Events

You can hold events or competitions in order to increase publicity. A 'green week' encouraging staff to walk or cycle to work, could get you publicity on local radio and newspapers, as could an open day, where you take local school children for tours. Or could you have a special exhibition? Offer to talk about your career or how to start a business at your local school's career event, and make sure you tell your local paper.

Competitions

Hold a competition – you will need to issue a couple of press releases – one to launch it, and the second to announce the winners.

Charity work

Do not hide your light under a bushel if your business is making a donation to charity. A press release is a great way to let people know about community service, whether you offer training or apprenticeships to students or sponsor a local sports team.

Seasons

You can also tie in a press release with a holiday or special occasion. Could your business do something related to Valentines Day, Fathers Day or Christmas?

Research

Statistics make a good basis for a press release. Do some market research with your customers about the latest styles or your new product.

✍👤 USEFUL RESOURCES: Awareness event finders

- www.woodlandsjunior.kent.sch.uk/customs/questions/specialdays.htm
  A fabulous site of awareness weeks, developed by a Kent school.

- www.bbc.co.uk/health/awareness_campaigns
  Health awareness events supported by BBC Health.

- www.expertsources.co.uk/forward_planner.asp
  Events list for members, membership from £30 annually.

✎ EXERCISE: Your press release

Note down your own ideas for press releases here:

_____

_____

_____

_____

_____

_____

_____

_____

_____

_____

_____

_____

_____

_____

_____

_____

_____

_____

_____

_____

_____

_____

_____

Photographs and images

Be prepared to provide photos to accompany your press release. A small image on the first page of a press release can attract a journalist's interest when they may otherwise pass it by.

If you sell products made by someone else, ask the manufacturer if they can let you have a selection of portrait and landscape product shots. If you create your own products you will need to provide your own photographs. Digital cameras have made it easier in many ways for amateurs to get good photographs. Use a well lit plain background: if you can, purchase a light tent, which will create a uniform background and diffuse the light. If you do not have one, use a thick piece of white/off white fabric as background (blackout fabric works well). Try dark and light backgrounds and see which ones show off your products the best. And buy the best camera you can afford. If using a digital camera make sure you have set it to take images at the highest resolution – see below for more on image size and resolution.

If you are not confident about photography you may need to find someone to take some shots for you. To keep the costs down you may be able to find an enthusiastic amateur or photography student. Ask them for a range of high resolution images (see below) if they are using a digital camera. Alternatively, you could ask someone to touch up or enhance your own images.

If you offer a service, it may be trickier to find suitable images. You could use photos of people using your service – make sure you have the subjects' permission before using their images for promotion. If you include a quote, you could offer photographs of the speaker.

Using digital images

Nowadays it is essential to be able to offer digital images to journalists, which you can email or send on a disc. Digital images on a website or in an emailed press release need to be of relatively low quality or resolution; about 72 dots per inch (dpi) or pixels per inch (ppi). This keeps the size of the email or file down – which is important as large emails or images on websites are slow to upload. Digital images for printing need to be 'high

Images on a website need to be of relatively low quality - about 72 dots per inch. Images for printing need to be 'high resolution' with a minimum of 300 dpi.

resolution', with a minimum of 300 dpi. The resolution/dpi indicates how many dots make up each tiny section of the image. The more dots per inch, the greater the detail and the clearer the photo. To find the resolution of your images, right click and select 'properties' which in most programs will tell you the image size and resolution. The number of dpi is dependent on the size of an image, so if your photo is 300 dpi but only 2cm wide, it will look very blurred or blocky if a magazine wants to reprint it at 5cm wide as the pixels will be spread over a greater area. Instead, for print purposes, aim for images which are 300-500 dpi and measure at least 10cm wide/high. You need to start with high resolution images, as while it is possible to reduce the quality, ie create a low resolution image from a high one, it is not possible to go the other way.

A program like Adobe Photoshop Elements will help you manipulate your images, change the background, optimise them for internet use or add watermarks to prevent people lifting them off your website and using them for their own purposes.

Most of the time you will want to include a small image in the main body of the press release. However, when sending in a sample or press pack you may want to offer further images, perhaps on a labelled disc. If you are sending prints, label them on the back using a sticky label. Include the title of the press release or products, your business name and contact details in case the photo gets separated from the press release. Never write on the back of photos – it will come through on the front.

✋ **HOW TO... Do it outdoors**
For good lighting, try taking photographs outdoors – natural light on cloudy day gives the best results.

Distributing your press release

You need to weigh up whether to email or post your press release. If you post it, you can guarantee how it will come out, eg colour printed, on good quality paper, and displaying the correct colours for your logo. A printed release is also essential when you send in a sample. However, nowadays many publications are entirely IT-dependent, and an email release will link the journalist swiftly into your website.

If you are sending your release by email, never send it as an attachment. Copy and paste your release into the body of the email, to make it easy for the journalist to see your story at a glance. Just by requiring them to click to open a document you are reducing the number of people who will look at your story, and your release will be more likely to fall prey to spam filters.

If posting a press release, it is important to get the formatting spot on. Number the pages, insert 'more/over' at the bottom if your text runs over more than one side, and staple pages together. There is nothing more frustrating for a journalist who wants to cover the story than to find that the second page with all the contact details on has got lost. Label samples and images accompanying the press release with your company name and contact details, again, in case they get separated (see pages 36-37 for how to format a press release).

Image: Most popular wooden toys Christmas 2007, Jane's Toys

Media Contact: Jane Porter, jane@janestoys.co.uk 07900 580668

↑ **Sample photo label, Jane's Toys**

✋ HOW TO...
Create press packs and samples

A press pack is a small folder including your press release plus additional information and samples. Sending a press pack by post may cost more, but it is a great chance to get creative. Think how you can make your pack stand out: you may be able to send samples to every journalist you want to contact, but if that is too costly, could you include sample fabrics or miniature versions instead?

Or why not include a 'pillow gift', anything from a small bar of chocolate up to a bottle of champagne? Do not be deterred if this is outside your budget, as journalists will still be interested in anything new or different even without a gift. If you have a small budget for samples, select a few publications where you would really like to feature, and call up and speak to the most appropriate journalist. Tell them what you have on offer and find out if they would just like a press release or if they need a sample. By doing this, you will be making sure that the samples you offer go to the people who will be really interested in them.

Press pack checklist

If posting a press pack, you may also want to include some or all of the following:

- A page about your company or your mini-biography
- Business cards
- A catalogue
- A CD of images
- Dates for forthcoming events where you are exhibiting or selling
- A page of your tips or a short article (see *Writing to promote your business*, page 66).

Keep written inclusions succinct and to a single side. Remember to include your logo and contact details on each sheet.

✏️ EXERCISE: Make your press pack

Reread the notes on the previous pages, and note down your ideas for items to include in your press pack here. Plan when you will send them out:

⌁🖱🕐 USEFUL RESOURCES:
Press release distribution sites

You can submit your press release to a range of organisations that are set up to distribute your release for you. Some of these are better than others. Some are totally free while others charge a small fee, and some have a US bias. It is worth trying them out to see which ones work for you.

The following mainly rely on journalists subscribing to their sites or visiting them to pick up news:

- www.pressbox.co.uk
- www.prweb.com
- www.prfree.com
- www.free-press-release.com
- www.responsesource.com (charges a small fee)
- www.emediawire.com
- www.clickpress.com

Write in further resources that you find useful:

The following send releases on your behalf to local, regional and/or national print and broadcast media, charging a couple of hundred pounds a time to distribute the release you have written.

- www.prnewswire.co.uk
- www.cision.com

Case studies – selling your own story

Sites like this are run by agencies or journalists in search of sensational true life stories to sell for magazines.

- www.cash4yourreallifestory.com (women's magazines)
- www.cash4yourstory.co.uk (newspapers)
- www.frontpageagency.co.uk
- www.photo-features.co.uk
- www.eanews.co.uk/stories.asp

🕐 **TWO MINUTE TIP**

If you are speaking to an editor, ask them whether they prefer to receive press releases on paper or by email. Note their preference in your contacts list.

🕐 **TWO MINUTE TIP**

Do not 'cc' people when sending a press release: it gives a much better impression if it looks like you have mailed the journalist individually.

Your notes

Your notes

Contacts

Making media contacts and building relationships is key to promoting your business. This section tells you how.

Making contacts

You need to build a list of contacts to send your releases to, and this will take time. Start local and small, as local media are most likely to be interested in your story and it is the perfect way to hone your release writing skills.

Always remember to get a specific named contact to target with your press release. A release addressed to a particular person will receive a lot more attention than a general release sent to the media outlet. Ring up the paper and ask, "Who's the best person to send information to about (your chosen topic)?" Add journalists' names and details to a 'contacts database' as you go along. This could be an address book, file cards, or you may prefer to set up a database on your PC.

A program like Excel is ideal for creating a contacts database. Set up columns for the name of the publication, the name of your contact, their job title, email, address and phone number.

There are some resources to help you build your contact lists. Books such as *The Writers' and Artists' Year Book*, *The Writers' Handbook* and the *Guardian Media Guide* all include a range of contacts in different sectors, but most are only updated annually and have just one or two contacts per publication. However, they are a good starting point for finding numbers to call for up-to-date named contacts, and cost less than £20.

It is also possible to purchase contacts databases which are regularly updated. ACPR offers up-to-date lists of contacts in specific media areas such as women's magazines, weddings, homes, etc. Prices start from around £50, making this an affordable way to get the right contacts, and saving you both time and money. Each database will cost less than buying the actual magazines and it is far quicker to click on the email addresses to send an email than to plough through magazines to try and find the right person.

Magazines rarely offer all the contact details you will need. Other companies such as List Logix and Romeike offer subscription services where you pay a monthly fee (several hundred pounds) for thousands of contacts across all UK media, either on a disk or more commonly now through their online services.

Magazine	Contact title	Contact name	Email	Address	Phone	Comments
Bella	Editor	Jayne Marsden	Editor @bauer.co.uk	H. Bauer Publishing Academic House, 24–28 Oval Road, London, NW1 7DT	0207 241 8000	weekly. (Tuesday) BC1C2 females aged 25-54 with children Circulation 331,534
	Acting Fashion Editor	Henny Letailleur	bella.fashion @bauer.co.uk			Acting fashion editor until further notice

⏱ TWO MINUTE TIP

When you send out your release, make sure you keep a record in your database of which journalists and publications contacted you about it. You may have found an ally for the future, or can avoid mailing people who have commented that they are not interested in your subject area.

You can also submit your releases to press release distribution websites. Many are free, some charge a nominal fee, and others rank your press release according to how much you pay. This is no replacement for using your own contacts list, but may help spread the word even further. (See *Useful resources* on page 43 for a list.)

Telephone calls

Making calls really helps you promote your business. It is more personal than an email, and harder to ignore. Here are some tips to help you make calls to boost the success of a press release, as well as advice on making promotional calls in general.

Think and plan your calls. Part of making calls is about building relationships with the right people.

Make a call before you send a press release, to check you are sending it to the most appropriate person and let them know that your info is on its way. You could start by asking, "Can I ask you a couple of questions now?" If they are rushing to meet a deadline and can't talk, you can fix up a time when they are likely to be more receptive. That is still a good outcome for the call, as they will now be expecting you to call back at the arranged time.

🖱① USEFUL RESOURCES: Media contacts

Directories which are updated annually:
- *Media Directory: The Essential Handbook* (Mediaguardian) £19.99
- *Writers' and Artists' Yearbook 2007* (A & C Black Publishers Ltd) £14.99
- *Writer's Handbook* (Macmillan) £14.99

Databases which are updated more regularly:
- ACPR: www.acpr.co.uk for databases for individual media sectors from £50
- List Logix: www.listlogix.co.uk from £600 annually for 'read only' access to £2,000 for UK contacts.
- BRAD: www.brad.co.uk 13,500 contacts available in print or online. £1,200+VAT for an annual subscription
- Mediadisk: www.romeike.com. Online or disk of contact information, news feed. Deliver and track press releases, record relationships with journalists from £2,400-3,600 per year

Write in further resources that you find useful:

_____

_____

_____

_____

✐ EXERCISE: Create your contacts

Think about how you will file your contacts. In an address book, on file cards, or on your computer? Set up the system that will be of most use to you, and spend fifteen minutes adding contacts each day until it is up-to-date and useable. See www.prbasics.co.uk for an Excel template you could use.

When you get someone who is free to talk, ask what sort of stories they are looking for. Try to find out how you can help. If you can immediately meet their needs, tell them all about what you have to offer. If what you have prepared does not tie in with what they are after, thank them for their time, and suggest that you will be back in touch when you have something useful for them. They will be left with the impression that you are trying to supply them with useful material, rather than just promote your business. With luck, they will also notice your name if you then email through a story, rather than deleting it straightaway.

The follow up call

Anything from a day to a week after sending the press release, make a follow up call. If you have written a good press release, the journalist may have all the details that they need. However, if they have looked at your release and discarded it, a phone call may not help. You will need some smart tactics to grab their interest and offer them something beyond what is written on a press release. Plan the questions you want to ask and have responses to different situations in mind. This will help you feel confident when making a call. Do not start by saying "Did you get my press release?" A journalist can easily dispatch you with a 'yes' or 'no'. Instead, you could remind them about who you are and the information you sent, "I'm calling from Jane's Toys, my name is Jane Porter. I was wondering what you thought about the press release I sent you yesterday about our unique range of fair trade wooden toys." Then you might want to check if it is a good time to talk.

Making the call

Before you start. Find out a little about the person you are calling – read the recent articles they have written, work out what they like to cover. Have your script and promotional materials in front

TWO MINUTE TIP
Set yourself a time slot each day for phoning, and discipline yourself to making calls for that hour or half hour.

of you. You may not need them, but it will help you remember your key points.

If your target journalist is not there, do not leave an answerphone message. Try asking the receptionist or a colleague if he or she knows when the journalist is likely to be at their desk – if you find out they only come into the office on certain days note it down in your contacts database for future reference and plan in a call at an appropriate time and day.

During the conversation. Smile. If you are smiling you will feel positive and confident and this will come across to the person at the other end of the line.

Use the person's name. This helps them feel like you are interested in them and not just calling all the journalists you can find.

Listen. When the journalist is talking, make sure you are paying attention rather than planning what to say next. Having a script in front of you will remind you what you need to say.

Focus on your goals for the conversation. Have them written down in front of you.

After you have hung up. Write up your call on your database of contacts. Take actions as soon as possible. If you are emailing more information or sending something in, do it right away.

Put in another call in your diary to follow up on further information requested or samples sent.

Now do the exercise opposite to plan your calls. Look at *The follow up call* for ideas to get you started.

TWO MINUTE TIP
It is fine to take a moment and make notes – ask the journalist to repeat what they said, if you need, and explain that you are noting it down. They will know that you value what they are saying.

✏ EXERCISE: Script your calls

Write down a good start for your call here:

_____

_____

_____

_____

Think about what you want to achieve from the call. Is it simply to find out if they will cover your item, or do you want to give them further good reasons as to why your products or services will be just what the readers want to find out about? What message do you want the journalist to take away from the call? Unless they have a lot of time you will only probably be able to get a couple of points across. You will want them to remember your company name or the name of your product, and what is new and unique about it. Focus on getting those points across first. Write down your goals for calling here:

_____

_____

_____

_____

What can you offer that will help the journalist? You cannot show your products over the phone, so make sure you have thought about samples and whether you can send them something. Or if you have a service, could you offer them the chance to experience it? Could you customise a press release to answer their particular questions or follow up on their interests, and tell them that you will send them some more, relevant information shortly? Can you see if they would like some high resolution images on a disc or by email? Take a few moments to note down what you have to offer journalists when speaking to them:

_____

_____

_____

_____

⇒ THINK ABOUT... Using your calling skills

The tips on these pages work when you are calling to promote your business to anyone. If you want to leave leaflets somewhere, you can make a call with that goal in mind. Just revise your script, and think about what you can offer each different group of people you are calling. If you are trying to get your products into stores, would an on-site event attract customers to their store? Can you do a special offer for their clients?

✏️ EXERCISE:
Make the most of cold callers

Next time some annoying company rings up to try to sell you something, do not hang up. Instead, analyse what they are doing and make notes.

Did they use your name? How many times?

What did they offer you first?

How did they try to sell it to you?

If you said 'no' to the initial offer, what was their response?

What annoyed you about the call?

Did you feel they were listening to what you said?

How could the call have been better?

Think about how you can use parts of their techniques to improve your phone manner.

Getting coverage locally

Targeting local media is a great way to get coverage for your business and increase sales to local people. Journalists from the local paper and radio station always need stories about the area, and there is less competition than at a national level.

Start with your local newspapers. Look in the paper for the list of staff to find names and addresses to send press releases to. As suggested in the previous section, *Telephone calls*, ring up and ask who covers the subject area most appropriate to your business or story. Aim to build a personal relationship with staff at the local paper, so you know the right person to get in touch with as soon as you have something new to tell them about your business.

Always make sure that your press release contains 'real news' that is relevant to the paper concerned. Have you bought copies of your local paper, and checked out the sort of stories they like to cover? (See the exercise on page 52.) Make sure you create a release that will be of interest to the paper's readers, and which is written in the style of the paper. Emphasise the local nature of your business and the topic of the release.

Check out the schedule for local paper lifestyle supplements. Is there a weekly review section you could submit something to? Or do they have different issues for spring wedding season or back

Aim to build a personal relationship with staff at the local paper, so you know the right person to get in touch with as soon as you have something new to tell them about your business.

> ⏱ **TWO MINUTE TIP**
> If you are not sure which papers cover your local area, search the databases at www.newspapersoc.org.uk.

Competition prizes are a great way to get publicity for minimal outlay. Collect addresses from entrants, and you can mail them again and generate more interest.

to school? These may be ideal targets for a press release or samples.

Perhaps get in touch to offer a competition for local readers as well. Prizes are a great way to get publicity for minimal outlay. Collect email or postal addresses from competition entrants, and you can mail them again and generate more interest. As they have entered the competition to win your product or service, you will know that they are people who are mostly interested in your products. (See page 74 for more on competitions.)

Investigate local specialist press too. Think your way into the mind of your customers, and this will help you work out what they are reading. If your product is aimed at young women, look to see if there are any free newsletters given out at the local train station or in bars or nightclubs. Think laterally. New home owners could also be getting married or

starting a family – why not check out the glossy local magazines you see in estate agents. All these magazines are in need of stories. And there may be local websites focussing on your area where you could get coverage, like the www.myvillage.com network.

If you see other businesses profiled in a magazine or newspaper or website that is read by prospective customers ring the editor of the publication and tell them why you should be covered as well. Alternatively add them to your list of publications to target.

Local radio

Local radio shows need people with interesting views. Make a point of listening to a local station if you do not normally tune in. Identify shows where they have guests, and think how you might be able

← Jane's Toys advert in local paper

⇒ **THINK ABOUT... What to say**

If you are successful in getting on the air, be prepared. Have three key points to get across. One of these points will probably be the name of your business or web address – repeat this more than once if you can! You are unlikely to get time for any more than three points unless you are in a longer discussion show.

to fit into their format. Ring up and find who you should speak to about guest appearances – you may want to start by asking for the producer of your chosen programme. Ask them about the sort of person they are looking for and the kind of story or topic they like to discuss. If you have an idea that meets their needs, tell them there and then. If not, find out whether they prefer to be contacted by phone, email or letter, and contact them when you have come up with something relevant.

Local advertising

You can supplement local PR with local advertising – and local newspaper editors may be more open to doing a feature on your business if you are advertising too. Advertising in the classified section of your local newspaper can be a relatively cheap but effective way of reaching potential customers. The Yellow Pages and Thomson directories offer free listings for businesses. Other places to advertise cheaply could include local schools' newsletters, and parish magazines. More people are running local magazines through franchise operations nowadays. These are commercial enterprises funded by advertising, so you are most likely to get editorial coverage if you pay for an advert too. However, it is also worth getting in touch to offer features on your area of expertise or 'top tips' in case they are seeking editorial.

Local events

Special events attract people to your business, and provide a good reason to issue a press release to local papers. Ideas include an open day, with a behind the scenes look at how your business runs, or a tour for school children. A 'green week' or similar event with a focus on recycling makes good publicity, or even a sale or special promotion on a range of products. You can also use your specialist expertise to gain free publicity. Offer your services as a speaker to local groups – anything from the WI to local business forums. People may be

interested in hearing how you have started your business, how you make your product, or about your particular services. If you make something, why not offer to do a demonstration. You could also sponsor a charity or fundraising event, or even a local team – football, darts, whatever appeals to you. Invite journalists who cover your area to these events or send them photos afterwards.

> **USEFUL RESOURCES: Local listings websites**
>
> - www.thebestof.co.uk
> - www.myvillage.co.uk
> - www.upmystreet.com
> - www.villagesonline.com
>
> Write in further resources that you find useful. Start in your library if you are not sure which listings and publications are available in your area:

Special events attract people to your business. Ideas include an open day, a tour for school children, a 'green week' or a sale or promotion on a range of products.

✏️ EXERCISE: My local media

Jot down a list of the local newspapers, magazines and radio stations that you are aware of. Then, pop down to the newsagents; check out local estate agents and the library and collect copies of all the local publications you can find. Ask friends who have lived in the area for a long time too, and search on the name of your town online. When you have a pile of papers, analyse them and answer the questions below.

Note down the contact details from the publication and then add them to your list of people to call. You can look at local radio shows in the same way.

Name of publication	Target audience	Relevant for promoting my business?	What ideas could I target them with?	Contact details

Your notes

Your notes

Your website

A website is essential for almost every business these days. Read this section to find out how to promote your site.

Have a website that works

A website is a great way to promote your business, and, if you are busy, a website will save you time and money too. A website never closes so you can tell people about your business and generate sales 24 hours a day, 7 days a week. Potential customers can find your contact details in an easy and convenient way, whenever they require, and you will reach customers who may never have found you in another way.

A well-designed website can promote and strengthen your company image; your customers will be able to immediately find out who you are and what you have to offer. If they do not find you online, there is always the danger that they will find your competitors. Your own domain name (for example, www.janestoys.co.uk) will establish your presence online and allows you to set up email addresses which are specific to your company. Jane@janestoys.co.uk appears much more professional than a hotmail or yahoo address.

What to include on your website

Your website should display all that your business offers in one convenient location for customers to browse at will. There is no need for them to wait for you to call them back. A website can replace a brochure for many businesses, and is easily updated with the latest examples of your work.

Answering frequently asked questions (FAQs) on your website can help you and your customers. If you have terms of ordering, delivery costs and methods etc, on the site, potential clients can find out exactly what you offer before entering into a transaction with you. You may also save time answering the same questions from different customers. Look at the exercise opposite to see what you could have on your site.

Design for promotion

It is entirely possible to create a website yourself, if you are willing to take the time to learn how to use a little HTML (the coding language that is used to set up websites) or one of the programs which are designed to help novices set up their own websites. The BBC website has some excellent straightforward advice if you want to do it yourself at www.bbc.co.uk/webwise. Whether you are designing the site yourself or getting someone to do it for you, you will need to think about promoting the site right from the planning stages.

✋ HOW TO... Stop the spam
Having your email address visible on your website can lead to more spam. Have a contact form instead – it will not stop spam altogether but prevents your address being harvested so easily.

✎ EXERCISE: Website essentials

Do you have a website? If not then run through this list to help you plan your website content. Or, if you have one already, check that it includes everything that you need. An Ⓛ after an item indicates that you are required to include this information **by law**.

	Do I need this for my site?
Every site will need:	
Home page: a few lines explaining what you offer	☐
About the business: background information and further details	☐

Terms and conditions including the following:

A statement that the UK law is applicable Ⓛ	☐
A statement explaining that the consumer is entering into a legally binding contract Ⓛ	☐
Details of the ordering process and what it involves Ⓛ	☐
To advise when in the order process the consumer commits to a purchase Ⓛ	☐
Information about the availability, delivery and dispatch of goods Ⓛ	☐
Information about substitutions in the event that goods or services are not available Ⓛ	☐
Information about withdrawal/cancellation rights Ⓛ	☐
The consumer's right to cancel – when buying online every customer can cancel as long as it is within 7 days of the goods being received Ⓛ	☐
A clear complaints procedure Ⓛ	☐
Policy on returning goods Ⓛ	☐

Privacy policy – whether you will sell or pass on personal details of your customers to other organisations including:

A data protection statement Ⓛ	☐
A privacy policy and information about security issues Ⓛ	☐
A cookie (unique identifier) policy Ⓛ	☐
An opt-in box for unsolicited email Ⓛ	☐

Contact page:

Full company details – name, a UK geographic address Ⓛ	☐
An email address Ⓛ	☐

Products/services page:

A description of the goods or services being sold Ⓛ	☐
Pricing information, inclusive of any delivery charges, taxes, etc Ⓛ	☐
Information about how long the offer or price applies Ⓛ	☐

Other details:

Any regulation or registration you or the business hold Ⓛ	☐
Any applicable Code of Conduct Ⓛ	☐
VAT number (if appropriate)	☐

...continued overleaf

You may also want to include some or all of the following: **Do I need this for my site?**

News page ☐

Sizes, measurements of products ☐

Newsletter ☐

Awards ☐

Media coverage

FAQs – frequently asked questions ☐

Testimonials ☐

Links ☐

Offers ☐

A blog ☐

If you want people to be able to buy your goods online you will also need a shopping cart system. ☐
This allows customers to look at your products and services, select them and buy/pay through your site.

If you have a product which is available to other businesses, you might want pages for:

Wholesale/trade terms ☐

Stockists ☐

And finally, you may want a program to count the number of visitors to your site, ☐
and analyse which pages they view, where they came from, etc. Examples include
Statcounter and Google Analytics, or it may be provided as part of your web hosting.

Getting a good website ranking

There are hidden factors that can affect your website rankings. Firstly, meta tags, which are part of the HTML code behind a website. Meta tags should include a good relevant title, a description and the keywords that are relevant to each page within your website. When devising your meta tags, only use words related to the product, and do not repeat the same word over and over. In general three repetitions is the maximum – any more and the site could be penalised by search engines. In a meta tag, you can maximise the effectiveness of your words by using the same word more than once, eg wooden toys traditional, rather than wooden toys, traditional toys. Note, more emphasis will be put on the keywords you have if there are fewer of them.

The most important meta tag is the title. Search engines give the most weighting to this. Get the keywords at the front of the title and do not overfill it as, again, the words that are there will affect your rating more. The title meta tag is also used in many search engines as the listing title. The description tag is the next most important. It is what the search engines display alongside the link to your website. No more than 250 characters long, it should contain your keywords / phrases and be interesting enough to attract the attention of the reader.

⇨ **THINK ABOUT... Ready made online stores**

There is no need to panic if you have no idea how to set up a website, and no budget for a designer. Millions of people like you now have their own online stores. Some set up an ebay shop, while others use companies like wahmshoppes.com or www.wahmall.co.uk who set up your store for you from their own template and host it for just a few pounds a month.

Meta tags describe your web pages, and 'alt tags' – a short description of the image which can be read by a search engine – do the same job for your images. Ideally get a keyword into the image tag where it makes sense to do so – remember that these image alt tags are shown by people with browsers who have images turned off (to speed up site download, etc) and are also read by screen readers for people with visual impairment.

Choosing the right keywords

Think about the keywords or phrases your potential customers will use when searching on the internet, and then ensure that the copy on your website is worded so that you use these in your main text.

Example: Keywords

It is good to use variations: for example, Jane is looking for customers who want wooden toys, so she would need to include phrases like:

- *Traditional toys*
- *Wood toys*
- *Wooden toys*

Jane then goes for more inspiration to a 'search term suggestion tool' which is a way to generate further possible search terms people might use. Search Google under 'search term suggestion tool' to help you find sites to develop your key search phrases or look for sites which indicate search term popularity.

When Jane uses the search term suggestion tool, it also suggests:
- *Toys for toddlers*
- *Wooden ride on and educational toys*
- *Child/children's toys*
- *Baby toys*
- *Wooden kitchen*
- *Wooden train.*

It also indicates which are the most commonly used search terms. Jane should try to use combinations of these terms when writing the pages for her website. It is important to be as

specific as possible, so that you get visitors to your site who are looking for the products you offer. In this case, Jane will not be using the suggestion for 'ride on' toys as she does not stock these. She will, however, now mention that she stocks toy wooden trains and wooden kitchen toys on her front page.

If you have the budget for it, a good web design company will give you professional advice about optimising your website to achieve the best search engine rankings, and will advise on submitting it to search engines and suitable directories. There are many guides to the technicalities available on the internet itself.

> ### ⏱ TWO MINUTE TIP
> Look back at the exercises earlier in the workbook on pages 9-12 for help with identifying your business keywords.

Promoting your business on the net

Publicising your website is an essential part of your business. Once you have a website, submit it to other relevant websites for inclusion in their directory, or ask them to swap links. Links between websites will not only be of use to your visitors, they are also important for your search engine rankings. Make sure that links to and within your website tell the search engine what it is linking to – do not simply say 'click here', instead use a keyword or phrase, for example 'website design by Glassraven'.

Reciprocal links are one of the most common and effective forms of website promotion. Links with complementary sites can lead to an increase in traffic for both websites. But, do not just do random exchanges and hope that this will help. Look for people selling products or services that will appeal to similar people, yet are different enough to your own product so as to avoid direct competition. Be picky too – make sure the site you propose to swap with looks as professional as your site, and gets a good number of visitors. Swapping links with sites with high page rank will be far more beneficial than swapping with sites with a low page rank. Google offers a tool called pagerank (see www.prchecker.info/check_page_rank.php) which tells you how highly their search engine rates each page in a site, giving you a rough idea on a scale of 1-10 of whether it has good incoming links, is getting many visitors and ranking well with search engines. Look for complementary businesses, whose customers might be similar to your target audience as these will have the most impact on your site rankings. Do not forget to look for local sites too which might have listings for local businesses, and other shopping directory sites. Try searching for your type of business and see where competitors are listed.

Once you have a list of sites you would like to swap links with, you need to prepare your link. Go back to your USPs (unique selling points) and the phrases you have come up with to sum up your business. Use these to come up with a concise phrase which you can supply to those businesses you want to swap links with. See the example for Jane's Toys, opposite:

✎ EXERCISE: A link for your business

Note down the key words you would like to describe your business here, then have a go at making a concise phrase to use for your link. You may need to edit it several times to cut out unnecessary words. Ask friends to have a look too:

Make a list here of the sort of sites you think might be good to link with for your business:

Example: Links

This is Jane's link: `Jane's Toys: Unique Fair Trade Wooden and Traditional Toys Next day delivery and gift-wrap service`

A short strapline telling potential customers what your business is about is ideal. Think about how you want the link to be worded and if you can, send the HTML code, for example

```
<a href="http://janestoys.co.uk">
<b>Jane's Toys: Unique Fair Trade
Wooden and Traditional Toys</b></a>
Next-day delivery and gift-wrap
service
```

to the site you wish to have a link on in order to get it exactly how you want it. Check that the link takes people to the page they are most likely to want, so Jane would probably take people to the page which has links to all the different sorts of toys she stocks – ie www. janestoys.co.uk/catalogue.htm.

You may also want a 'banner' with your logo on for link swaps. Some sites want text-only links, while others will allow you to supply a banner, a image which includes your logo and a few key words describing your business. Clicking on the banner will lead people to your site. You can design a banner yourself or get a web designer to make one for you.

Now you have your link wording and possibly a banner, contact the webmaster of the sites you would like to swap with, and say that you would like to include a link on a specific page on their site - would he or she be prepared to include a link to your site too? Explain how your sites could complement each other. Find out what size they wish the banner to be. If the link goes ahead, plan to check it every now and again to make sure both links still work.

↑ **An example of a banner**

🕐 **TWO MINUTE TIP**
The two most common banner sizes are a long thin banner at 468 x 60 pixels and a smaller button image at 120 x 60 pixels.

More website promotion

There are many more free or low-cost activities that you can do to boost traffic to your website. Here are several to get you started, and there is a checklist at the end of this section for you to make your own web action plan.

Update your content regularly

When people have visited your site once, what will attract them back? It can take several visits before people commit to a purchase. So it is important to keep the site updated regularly. Build interest and demand by promoting forthcoming updates, new products and sales in advance. Flag them up on your site, and have a way for people to subscribe for updates and reminders from your business. Once they have registered you can send them your newsletter (see page 70), or contact them with details of new offers and promotions – but remember to offer an 'opt out' (a quick way for them to say they do not want to receive further updates) on your newsletter in order to comply with rules on 'spam' email. Plan seasonal special offers, add interesting articles regularly, and tell your customers. Make sure you can keep up the commitment to update your site – nothing is worse than out-of-date information. Think about whether you want monthly or quarterlyupdates, and plan ahead. Updating your content regularly also encourages search engines to visit more frequently which in turn may raise the ranking of your site. A blog (see next page) with information about your site, and internal links to your site pages, may also be a good way of doing this.

🕐 **TWO MINUTE TIP**
Before you put time and effort into any of these tools, plan in time to update them. Pick one day each week as update day, perhaps.

USEFUL RESOURCES: Business websites

General business websites
- www.startups.co.uk
- www.ukbusinessforums.co.uk
- www.aardvarkbusiness.net
- www.smallbusinesssuccess.biz

Women's business websites
- www.everywoman.co.uk/networking
- www.motheratwork.co.uk
  (see Services and Information Directory)
- www.womenatwork.co.uk
- www.network.auroravoice.com

Write in more resources you find useful:

Use forums and newsgroups

If you want people to seek out your website, become an online expert in your subject. Participate in forums that relate to your product area, and contribute to relevant newsgroups. Consider submitting short articles or tips relating to your products or services. People are more likely to read an article than an advertisement and will often follow links from the article back to your site for more information. Make sure that your article contains useful information and is not just promotional blurb. People like to get advice from an expert – so will know that you are the person to ask about slings, for example, if they have read your article.

Join small business forums too. Check out the rules about advertising your business as each forum differs. Some are specifically set up to provide a directory of products and services or link up members with potential purchasers. Others are set up to support people in the same situations – for example, working from home. Mention your site as much as you can – offer help and advice, and you will get a good name, and referrals too. Word of mouth is one of the best ways to increase visits to your site.

New media promotion

The internet has a far wider range of ways to communicate with people than it did a few years ago. It is worth trying out different tools each month, telling people what you are doing through forums and your newsletter, and seeing which ones attract visitors to your site and lead to sales.

Blogs

A blog (or web log) is an online diary and can be a great way to build relationships with customers and potential clients. While customers may not be interested in the ins and outs of your personal life, it is worth thinking about whether you can provide something unique and interesting which will draw in new visitors and attract customers back for repeat visits. A blog contains text, images, and links to other blogs, web pages, and other media related to its topic. You should link from your website to your blog and back again.

When planning a blog, think how often you will update it, and stick to this plan. You need regular fresh content to get repeat visitors to value your site. Make sure you include a selection of images every so often, easy if you are commenting on products. If relevant, include links to other good websites. A selection of quality links will make your blog rank more highly, but do not add irrelevant links just for the sake of it.

THINK ABOUT... Top Tips

Think about your area of expertise – can you create regular tips that will be useful to others? Why not feature these on your blog or website, for example, news on Monday, your tips on Wednesday, and celebrity links to your products on Fridays.

Other social media

You can also create a podcast, which is an audio file containing a spoken message or programme. If you had some tips or thoughts to share you could record them onto your PC, and link to the broadcast from your website or blog. Similarly, sites such as Youtube.com allow you to create small videos and put them up on the internet. And virtual communities like Myspace.com give you the opportunity to create a page which can have lots of information about and links to your business. To create mini magazines which can be downloaded to mobile phones, visit: www.tocmag.com. This sort of technology allows small business owners to share their expertise in increasingly diverse and creative ways, and reach new customers. However, each one will take some time to create and a blog or Myspace site will also need regular updates. As before, out-of-date information does nothing for your business.

Really Simple Syndication

One more technological breakthrough is the RSS feed. This is a little piece of software that allows people to get automatic updates when you put something new on your site or blog. On web pages, web feeds (RSS or Atom) are typically linked with the word 'Subscribe', an orange rectangle, 🔲, or with the letters **RSS** or **XML**. The regular updates to your content will also help with your site rankings. See if you or your web designer can add one to your site.

Checklist for promoting your website:

Make a note of which tools to try and add them to your promotional plan. If you are planning on your computer, you may want to add another section to your plan for website promotion.

Look at your text and meta tags and see if you are including your keywords ☐

Create a strapline and banner ☐

Check your links every month or two and add new ones ☐

Join business forums ☐

Join forums relevant to your business area ☐

Write articles and tips ☐

Plan special offers for your site ☐

Add RSS feed ☐

Set up a page on Myspace.com ☐

Set up and maintain a blog ☐

Create a podcast ☐

Create a video for Youtube.com ☐

🖱🔊 **USEFUL RESOURCES: Blogging**

- www.blogger.com
- www.typepad.com
- www.livejournal.com
- www.blog.co.uk

Write in more resources you find useful:

_____

_____

_____

Your notes

Your notes

Writing to promote your business

Writing articles is a great way to promote your business. It costs nothing but a little time. Read on to find out how to improve your writing.

It is easy to feel daunted by the thought of writing an article but it is a great way to publicise your business. Many magazines and websites are glad to be offered free content and will snap up your piece for publication, and you will get a by-line and link through to your website into the bargain – instant publicity.

The best way to get started is to come up with a few ideas for articles. Many glossy magazines work about three months in advance – so plan ahead, especially if you are considering writing something with a seasonal theme. It is always helpful to check out any publication guidelines from the magazine or site about length, style, etc. Many publications only want articles that have not been published elsewhere, or they may only accept articles that are of a certain length.

Depending on the length you are aiming for, scope out between 3 and 10 points to cover. Think about writing a short article about something that you are an expert on – how to choose the best baby gear or childcarer, etc… or whatever your product or service is. This is a good way to generate coverage for your business, and will get you known as an expert in the field.

Example: Writing articles

Jane is planning on writing about her tips on choosing toys for different ages. She's going to use this in a pre-Christmas newsletter specially for people who have used her gift service.

Her initial ideas:
- *Toys for boys, toys for girls*
- *What to get at different ages*
- *Examples of bestsellers from her website*

With a little more thought, she decides to structure her article, so people can easily skim to the right age group:
- *Introduction – why people have difficulty choosing the right toys, a few key tips, and how this article will help*
- *Toys for babies under one*
- *Toys for pre-schoolers*
- *Toys for primary school children*

After each section, Jane will have some links to 'toys for boys' and 'toys for girls' in the appropriate age group. At the end, she will sum up with a few more general tips and a reminder of the postal dates for Christmas.

 THINK ABOUT... PR strategy
Tie your promotions in with your overall PR strategy and press release your promotion to all relevant media.

✏ **EXERCISE: Write an article**

Note down some ideas here for topics you could write about. What have you trained or qualified in? What skills do you use every day – could you write an article about using some of those skills for a business audience? What advice do you give customers when you sell to them? Could this advice be turned into an article? Could you come up with a 'how to' guide to make something? If you are still struggling, ask helpful friends and family what they think you are an expert on.

Now, pick one of your ideas, and expand it. Jot down some notes on what you would like to cover in the article. Note down as many points as possible, add to them and expand on a few details. Use the space below to rearrange them so that they follow in a logical order, delete bits that become unnecessary, and you will soon be on your way to writing your first article:

Introduction

Idea 1

Idea 2

Idea 3

...continued overleaf

More ideas

Ideas for the conclusion

Know your target audience

Now you have a framework for the article, pause before you get stuck into writing, and think about who you are writing this article for. If it is for your own website or newsletter go right ahead, as you are the one who decides on style and content. Remember who your target audience are, and focus the article on what they might want to know, in language they would use.

However, if you want someone else to publish an article, they will have ideas about the length, style and content too. So you need to pitch your idea to the editor of your target publication. Start by reading the publications you would like to write for before you pitch, and check that they have not had a similar article in recent months. Think about the topics they cover and the style the publication is written in, and tailor your 'pitch' accordingly. You can pitch by phone or email. Email is often the best way to contact an editor initially, but always follow up by phone. In the email, you need to explain your idea, why it is new or unique, and how it will appeal to the readers. Emphasise your specialist knowledge and why you are a good person to write this feature.

 **Example: The pitch**

Jane is contacting her local parenting magazine. Here is her letter and pitch:

Dear Fiona,

I have an idea for an article which would be just right for your December issue. It is always difficult to choose the right toy to give. My article will look at which toys are best for which age groups. I will give examples of the latest trends and lasting classics, and a range of places to buy, both locally and by mail order.

I've been selecting toys for my store for several years now, so I have inside information on what sells, and always get feedback on what has been a hit from my regular customers.

I'll give you a ring in the next couple of days to see if you are interested.

Best Wishes, Jane.

> ⏱ **TWO MINUTE TIP**
> Get someone else to read the article too. They will probably spot typos that you have missed. Ask them to highlight where they would like more information.

✎ EXERCISE: Fine-tune your pitch

Now, jot down the key points of your article. What is unique about it? Do you have great case studies to illustrate it? And have you got specialist knowledge to share? Write your pitch here:

After fine-tuning your pitch, make sure you know who to send it to. With a small publication or website there may be only one editor to contact, but check that you are contacting the right person at larger magazines and newspapers. A call to the editor's PA or switchboard may be all you need to find the best contact.

Once you know which publication you are writing for, you need to focus the article accordingly. If you are writing for your own site or newsletter, your article should be aimed at your customer – perhaps focus on how you can solve a problem for them. If writing for another publication, think about what their readers want to know.

🕐 TWO MINUTE TIP

One side of text in a magazine is usually about 800 words – and web articles are usually best kept even shorter – 400 to 800 words maximum.

🖱🔊 USEFUL RESOURCES: Article publication

There are a few groups dedicated to spreading articles for publication for free on newsletters and websites. Many of these are US-based, so check which ones will reach your target audience.

- Article Depot: www.articledepot.co.uk
- Article Announce: www.web-source.net/articlesub.htm
- IdeaMarketers: www.ideamarketers.com
- Publisher Network: groups.yahoo.com/group/publisher_network

Write in more resources you find useful:

⇨ THINK ABOUT... The follow-up call

When you do call to follow up your pitch, first of all check if it is a good time to talk – and if not, arrange a time to call back when it is more convenient. Remember, even if the editor does not like the idea you suggest, you can ask them what they are looking for, and get some valuable feedback which will help you develop your next idea.

⏱ **TWO MINUTE TIP**

Write a short paragraph about yourself and your product/services – approximately two lines which the magazine can use as a footnote to your article. This is your advertisement, so put as much work into this as the rest of the article, using your USPs from earlier in the workbook.

When you are writing, do not stop to think about whether you have got the perfect phrase. Just write. When you finally come to a halt having written something on each of your points, print out a copy and read it through. Use a pen to make changes. You may want to alter the order of your points after you have read the article as a whole.

The same technique will improve your leaflets and other literature. Note down what you want to say in point form, prioritise it, fill in each point, then go back and trim it down. Remember, when writing for leaflets, people need to be able to see your key points at a glance. Fewer words are better.

You need to negotiate the terms under which your article will appear. Larger publications will expect to pay several hundred pounds per thousand words to professional journalists, and you are doing journalists a disservice if you say, "I do not need payment" if it is offered. However, many websites and smaller publications are keen to fill their pages and may offer advertising space or a mention for your business underneath the article. Others will even want you to pay to get your article printed – this is called 'advertorial' and will be marked as a 'promotion' above the article so readers know you have paid for the space. Consider the outcome you want when calling publications.

Newsletters

A newsletter can help increase visitors to your website, and when you are producing a newsletter, you are also generating new content for your site. You do not have to be a writer to produce a newsletter. Provided you are competent with English, you can produce a helpful publication, with news about your products and services. A newsletter will remind people about your website on a regular basis, and also develop a relationship with your clients and potential customers. Ask visitors to your site to subscribe, so you can email your newsletter to them without being guilty of spamming. If you are not clear, spam is email sent to people who have not asked to receive the information. Spammers collect email addresses and send out mailshots in bulk.

If you have planned out the activities for your business over the coming year, you are partway towards planning your newsletter. Use the newsletter to announce new products, and when you update your site. If you can, include an article on a relevant subject, or some news stories. A newsletter is a good place to announce a competition. You will be building loyalty amongst people who are already interested in your product.

Microsoft Word is fine to design a basic newsletter. Microsoft Publisher contains ready made templates, and is ideal if you want to create a print newsletter, and if you are web-savvy you could create your own HTML newsletter template. See *Useful resources* for suggestions for tools to help you send your newsletter online.

⇒ **THINK ABOUT... Writing regularly**

Try to write an article or simple 'top ten tips' every month to build up the list of things you have written. Aim to have articles on a number of websites, and you may find people will contact you for a comment or quote or product reviews in your area of expertise. Add the articles to your website, and put on other tips to attract people to use your site. By building up a library of tips and articles you will attract people back time after time.

✏ **EXERCISE: Your newsletter**

How often will you send a newsletter?
- Monthly
- Bi-monthly
- Quarterly

Note down some ideas for topics you could write about each issue:

🖱① **USEFUL RESOURCES: Newsletters**

- Yahoo Groups: http://groups.yahoo.com/ Set up your own mailing list to which users can subscribe.
- Constant Contact: www.ConstantContact.com US-based subscription service for email newsletters.

Write in more resources you find useful:

Making newsletter contributions

You can also contribute to someone else's newsletter. Newsletter editors are always looking for good content, as it is hard to produce all the content they need on their own, and most cannot afford to pay for it. In exchange for allowing your content to be published for free, the newsletter editor should give you a 'by-line' and link to your site for free. If this seems like a lot of hard work, remember that you can use the article in other ways – on your own site or newsletter, or offer it to several different newsletters or sites with different readerships. Search for as many potential sites to place your article as possible. Large newsletters tend to only accept articles that have not already been widely published, so target them first. Smaller ones may not be as picky. Take a few minutes to search for other businesses which offer newsletters. Subscribe to them and keep an eye out for ones which might accept an article from you.

A newsletter will remind people about your website on a regular basis, and also develop a relationship with your clients and potential customers.

Your notes

Your notes

Special offers

Special offers are a great way of drawing attention to your business and attracting new customers. This section looks at different types of promotion, and how to maximise their effect.

Special offers for promotion

Before you decide on a promotion, take time to work out what you want your promotion or offer to achieve. Do you want sign ups for your newsletter, to attract new users, to reward current customers, or get them to buy again? Note down your objectives and when you are developing your promotional ideas check to make sure that they meet your goals. If, for example, you want to increase the number of people visiting your website, make sure that you publicise your promotion beyond your existing customers. If, however, you are looking to build loyalty amongst your clients, devise special offers exclusively for them. Many businesses find that they get most of their business from a small group of loyal customers who purchase repeatedly.

Think about how many different promotions you can afford to offer throughout the year. Consider seasonal themes such as Easter, summer holidays, back to school, etc, and promotional weeks or months too (look back at the twelve-month promotional plan earlier in the workbook for more ideas).

Explore cross promotion with a non-competing company selling to your target market. This could be a link with a magazine or website, or another shop or online store. You could make a competition exclusive to their members, or offer a discount or freebie to people quoting a code. Offer codes help you establish how many people are coming to your site through each promotion. Work out the finances for each offer. Know how much profit you make on your products, and how much of this you can afford to give away. Consider the value of advertising compared to the amount each promotion will cost you. For example, if an advert in a magazine costs £200, why not offer the magazine competition prizes instead which could cost you less and get better publicity. Your business will have editorial promotion in the magazine, and you may also get contact details for all the entrants, giving you a valuable mailing list.

Competitions

Prize draws are the most popular form of competition. Ask entrants to answer a simple question about your products or services. Think about how competition entrants could help you, and what would make them feel more involved with your business at the same time. You could ask them to name a new product, tell you their views, or write a slogan, or have a virtual treasure hunt to entice people to look around your site.

Pick a prize that will appeal to potential customers, as they are the people you are trying to attract. If you do not have a prize to give away, another company may offer promotional goods as prizes. Why not link up with someone else with an appropriate client base and offer your product as a prize on their

 THINK ABOUT... PR strategy
Tie your promotions in with your overall PR strategy and press release your promotion to all relevant media.

✋ HOW TO... Make your customers work for you

Customers are your most cost-effective advertisers. If they are pleased with your products or services they will recommend you. You can encourage them to do this with referral incentives. Send a special offer voucher with your orders to promote returning custom, or provide a referenced leaflet with your customer's name on and ask them to distribute it in return for a free item if someone orders quoting their name.

site, and vice versa. You could also get promotional items made up. If you can come up with something that your customers, or their children, will value, customise them with your web address and you will get ongoing advertising. Send users an email when they enter, and offer a discount as a 'thank you' and an extra incentive to buy.

Rules

All promotions need rules. Before you promote a competition, decide if it is open to UK residents only; if people can enter only once per person/email address/postal address; and if you will disqualify people who bend the rules. Ensure rules are clear and accessible to everyone. Explain that you will disqualify 'automated/bulk entries and entries from third parties'. If you want people to purchase in order to enter the competition, include an element of skill such as a tiebreaker or slogan. Otherwise, you cannot limit entries to those who are buying. Let people know if you make changes to your

You could ask competition entrants to name a new product or write a slogan, or have a virtual treasure hunt to entice people to look around your site.

competition while it is running. Explain the changes on your site and email previous entrants. Quizzes will require someone to check all the answers. Make sure you have an independent adjudicator.

Pick winners at random. Do not just pick the first unless your rules state that is how winners will be picked. Announce the winner on your website. This shows site users that the prize was won, gives them confidence in your website, and encourages them to trust your business. Inform the winner by email, and send the prize out as soon as possible.

✏️ EXERCISE: Special promotions planning

Think about potential competitions, promotions and special offers.

Who do you want to target?
- Existing customers
- Potential new clients
- Other:

_____

_____

_____

...continued overleaf

What do you want to achieve with the promotion?

• Sign ups for your newsletter?

• To reward current customers?

• To get customers to buy again?

• To increase the value of each customer's spend?

• Your own ideas:

What promotions or competitions could you run?

What prizes or incentives could you offer? Pick products that have a high mark up or minimal cost to you. Note down some ideas.

If you want people to increase their spend, what could you offer them if they increase their order value to, say, £25, or £50?

• An extra product

• Free postage?

• Insert your own ideas here:

How will you let people know about your competitions or offers?

Look at your promotion plan. Can you add a note in to mention these special promotions in your newsletter or on fliers? Insert your ideas here:

Your notes

Evaluating your progress

It is essential to find out what sort of promotion works best for your business. This section tells you how

Media coverage - it doesn't stop there

When you have written and sent out your press release, you will soon find you start getting some coverage for your business. If a journalist confirms that they are covering your story by phone or email, note down when the feature will appear, and make sure you get hold of a copy. A few publications will send you a complimentary copy of the magazine, but you should not rely on this so plan to buy a copy.

Sometimes a publication will give you a short mention without telling you. In one way you can look on this as an endorsement of your press release writing skills, as you included everything they wanted to know. In another way of course, it is a nuisance, as you will not be aware that the coverage is coming up. It really helps if you have a 'where did you hear of us?' box on your order form, or ask every customer who rings up with an order or query. That way you can sometimes pick up a media mention. When you have a large budget for promotion, you may want to use a media monitoring service. This is a service where another company scans all the media for selected key words, such as your company name. It costs from £100+ per month.

All your media coverage is extremely valuable to your business, long after the publication has been thrown away. Keep copies of each article. Scan them into your computer if possible. You can then use them on your website, or in your wholesale brochure. Pull out complimentary phrases and use them together with the name of the publication and date on your publicity materials. If you have a website, have a page for media coverage too. And if you have premises, enlarge the feature and display it. The coverage will add credibility and encourage retail and wholesale customers to buy. After all, a third party, the journalist, has reviewed your business and liked it. Make the most of your media coverage – do not just tear it out and then leave it in a drawer.

Evaluating your business promotion

Measuring what works helps you plan where to go next with promotion and advertising, and can save you time and money. It is hard to improve on what you are doing unless you learn what works and what does not. Ideally, think about how you will evaluate your promotion before you start. Make sure that you have your business's objectives in mind when planning your promotional activities, and then you can see whether the coverage you get contributes to achieving those goals. The diagram opposite illustrates this process.

In public relations, one way to assess the success of a campaign is to measure the number of column inches of coverage that you achieve in magazines and newspapers, and then calculate the equivalent cost of an

---

🕐 **TWO MINUTE TIP**
Set aside a few minutes at the same time every week to look over your promotional activities and see which ones are producing results.

advertisement of that size in the same place. This might tell you that you have saved a few hundred pounds or even a few thousand pounds, but it does not really get to the bottom of the effect of the promotional activity.

What you actually need to assess is the impact on your business of the activity. Have more people requested information, visited your website, or actually bought from your business? What goals did you have in mind when you planned the activity, and have they been met?

Earlier, we looked at goal or target setting, and discussed making the objectives SMART – Specific, Measurable, Achievable, Realistic and Timely (see page 15). When you get to the stage of evaluating your activity, you will realise just how useful a good objective is, and equally, it will become clear if your targets were vague or unrealistic.

Some things are easy to measure, and can be done using simple techniques or tools. Others, such as measuring changes in how people perceive your business can take more time or cost more. However, for small firms there are a number of ways to get started with measuring the value for money and success of your business promotion activities.

The simplest method is to ask everyone where they heard of you when they sign up for a newsletter or place an order. You can feed this information into a database, or if you only have a very small business, just keep a tally so you know the best places to promote your business. Build asking where people found your business into your telephone script, ordering process or website, so it happens automatically.

> ⇨ **THINK ABOUT... Simple surveys**
> A simpler way may be to just ask people's opinions when developing promotional materials, and then get their feedback on the finished item, be it a flyer or a feature in the local paper. If you are targeting mums, then show them some coverage and ask them what stands out about it and whether it encourages them to buy from you. Also ask what it does not tell them — that way, you can emphasise those points next time.

While many magazines or newspapers will notify you that they are covering your business, others may use information from a press release without contacting you. By monitoring where enquiries have come from you may discover fresh media coverage. If a publication proves a good source of contacts or orders, you can target then with further press releases, see if they would like to run a competition or other promotion, or think of taking out advertising.

Example of a simple tally count of orders resulting from media coverage:

Media	Number of orders	Total
Local paper	IIIII III	8
Article in specialist website	III	3
Trade magazine	IIIII IIIII IIIII IIIII	20

1 Audit
Where are we now?

2 Setting objectives
Where do we need to be?

3 Strategy and planning
How do we get there?

4 Ongoing measurement
Are we getting there?

5 Results and evaluation
How did we do?

Source: CIPR

Example: Which promotions worked?

If you want a more accurate analysis, you will need to take into account the costs of the promotion, and the amount of profit you make. In this example, Jane has been trying out various ways to promote her toy business. This example assumes she costs her time at a nominal £10 per hour.

Jane is surprised at her results, and there are a number of things she has learnt. She thought that the local paper might work well for her business, but taking into account the time she spent, it didn't make much profit. However, the journalist was interested in her business and will include some recommendations for toys at

Christmas. Jane is going to give it another try, as sometimes customers need to see a business as many as seven times before they actually commit to a purchase.

She decided to get a PR firm to target some national and trade publications for her, as she thought it was important to make the most of the run up to Christmas. The company sent out the press release in the summer, as many magazines work three or more months in advance. Jane got some coverage in a national women's weekly. She was disappointed that not many people ordered and their orders were of low value. She is going to think carefully before targeting consumer magazines again, and look more closely at the type of people who read the

PROMOTION	COST OF PROMOTION	RESULTS	EVALUATION
Local paper	Two hours work writing a press release, plus £5 for envelopes, paper, stamps etc. Total cost £25	• Increase in visitors to website over week of publication approx 5% • Three orders Total profit from all orders £24	Average order profit £8 Value of orders less cost of promotion = -£1
National consumer magazine mention	Public relations company to promote Jane's business for her. £250	• Increase in visitors to website over week of publication approx 20% • Twelve orders Total profit from all orders £60	Average order profit £5 Value of orders less cost of promotion = -£190
Article in trade publication	Public relations company to promote Jane's business for her. £250	• Increase in visitors to website over week of publication approx 20% • Ten orders Total profit from all orders £400	Average order profit £40 Value of orders less cost of promotion = £150
Article on family website	Four hours writing an article for the website. £40	• Increase in visitors to website over week of publication approx 100% • Seventeen orders Total profit from all orders £170	Average order profit £5 Value of orders less cost of promotion = £130

magazine as maybe her toys were more costly than the readers of this publication could afford. Trade publications were included on the suggestion of the PR company. Jane ships in a unique line of toys from India. A toy trade publication picked up on this story and ran a double page spread. As a result Jane is now supplying the toys wholesale to a number of other businesses. This is a great outcome and Jane is now looking again at the way her business is heading. She may move more into wholesale, as the larger order values make it more worthwhile.

Jane also wrote an article about toys for giving at Christmas for a parenting website. Because this contained a direct link to her website, and was mentioned in their newsletter, she got lots of click-thrus and a good number of orders. She is looking at more ways to work with this and other parenting websites.

This basic sort of analysis looks at the direct benefits to a business. It does not look at the longer term benefits to your business. If you have done a survey when planning your business, you will have some ideas about people's opinions, and you may want to follow up with regular surveys. If you are building up a database of customers and enquirers this can be used to find out what people think, whether they have seen any of your promotional activities, and whether they have encouraged them to purchase.

The benefit of regular surveys is that you can measure the effect of promotions. Be cautious as this can be costly and time consuming if you are surveying large numbers of people. Make sure you target the right groups. If you have been promoting your products in women's magazines, survey women rather than men. You need to be timely – a promotion may have a short-lived effect and you need to find out people's views before they forget.

✐ EXERCISE: Evaluating your promotion

You need to go back to your promotion plan to do this exercise. The empty seventh column is there so you can write by each promotional activity how you will measure its effects. Look at the ideas above, and see which ones will be best for each activity.

Month	Events	Activities	Targets	PR	Target Media	Evaluation
April	Real Nappy week	Stall at local NCT fair for parents to sign up for info	Local parents	Posters, leaflets, press release	Local paper	Aim: to get more local parents' details. Success measure: 25 new contacts Extra objective: 5 sales on the day, 10 sales over the next 2 months
May	Product available in new colour range	Competition to win new colour product	Parents, existing website customers	Press release, Newsletter to existing customers	Parenting magazines and websites	Increase in visitors to website by 20% over month of competition. Increase in sales sales by 2 a day.

Your notes

Your notes

How have you done?

Now you have reached the end of the book, review how far you have come. If at the start of the book you were unsure about where or how to begin, look at the questions opposite and mark where you feel you are now on each measure.

I feel confident about promoting my business:

Not at all confident   1 2 3 4 5 6 7 8 9 10   Very confident

I have clear objectives for my business:

No objectives   1 2 3 4 5 6 7 8 9 10   Well-defined objectives

I know who I am targeting with my promotion:

I'm very unsure   1 2 3 4 5 6 7 8 9 10   I know who I am targeting

I have clear plans for promoting my business:

No plans at all   1 2 3 4 5 6 7 8 9 10   Clear, well thought out plans

I am confident about writing a press release:

I'm very unsure   1 2 3 4 5 6 7 8 9 10   I can write a press release

I am confident about making telephone calls to promote my business:

Not at all confident   1 2 3 4 5 6 7 8 9 10   Very confident

I know about my local media and how to use it for promotion:

I know nothing about my local media   1 2 3 4 5 6 7 8 9 10   I know all about my local media

I am confident about promoting my business on the internet:

Not at all confident   1 2 3 4 5 6 7 8 9 10   Very confident

I am confident about writing to promote my business:

Not at all confident   1 2 3 4 5 6 7 8 9 10   Very confident

I know how to evaluate which promotions work well for my business:

I have no idea what works well   1 2 3 4 5 6 7 8 9 10   I am clear what works well

Now compare this to your answers on page seven. You should be feeling more confident and have plenty of ideas and plans for promoting your business and reaching more customers.

If there are areas where you still need help, make a plan to address them. Look for business books on the topic, talk to BusinessLink, or find out about local training courses.

You can also get in professional help, or sign up for email support from ACPR, where you get someone to answer your questions about PR by email any time you need.

Do not put this book away. There's an action plan overleaf which will remind you of lots of the activities you could be getting on with. Just spend 15 minutes each day on one action that you have planned, and your business will succeed and grow.

Email antonia@acpr.co.uk if you want to talk to me about business promotion. Best wishes for a successful future with your business.

Action plan

This worksheet sums up lots of the ideas outlined in the book, and has space for you to make notes as you work through each idea. Use this, or create your own action plan.

Action	Who/when? Note down who to target and/or when you plan to do the activity.
Set up database to monitor where enquirers/ customers find your business.	
Print business cards and hand them out.	
Devise a sentence to sum up your business, and practise it on anyone who asks 'what do you do?'	
Write a list of ideas on which to base a press release.	
Ask others what's unique about your business. Ask your customers about the publications they read and the websites they visit.	
Start a list of national and local publications to target. Collect newspapers and magazines.	
Make contacts at your target publications: phone journalists and ask them about the type of story they are interested in.	
Listen to a local radio station to find shows you could contribute to, promoting your expertise.	
Work out whether you could afford to offer a competition to one of your target publications.	
Look for local groups where you could do a talk or demonstration, call and offer your services.	

Action	Who/when?
	Note down who to target and/or when you plan to do the activity.
If you do not have one, plan a website.	
Find out about 'Search Engine Optimisation' to ensure that search engines can find you easily and link potential customers to you.	
Make a list of other websites that complement yours to swap links with. Do you have a 'banner' you can send to them? Swap email signatures too.	
Plan regular updates to your site to keep people coming back.	
Have a space on your website for people to sign up for updates about your business.	
Submit your website to online shopping sites, business directories and local websites.	
Look into online ads, such as Google adwords, Espotting, Overture and Mirago ads.	
Plan a newsletter to send out regularly to keep old customers and potential new ones interested.	
Plan a programme of special offers.	
Post special offers or new product promotions on relevant forums.	

Action	Who/when?
	Note down who to target and/or when you plan to do the activity.
Use your existing customers. Enclose a reorder form with their goods, and offer incentives so they recommend you to friends.	
Network – look for local business or women's groups.	
Look on the internet for relevant chat groups and forums – online networking can help build business contacts and reach potential customers.	
Write an article and use it in your newsletter.	
Offer the article to another website to use in their newsletter or on their website.	
Look for other complementary businesses and swap leaflets and promotional materials.	
Online auctions can attract new customers – think creatively about what you can auction to attract people.	
Send letters and samples to prospective clients.	
Sell at shows, shopping centres, craft fairs.	
Follow up enquiries that have not lead to an order – if you understand why people do not order you will be able to improve what you offer.	

Action	Who/when? *Note down who to target and/or when you plan to do the activity.*

Your notes

Your notes

Your notes

Your notes

Your notes

Your notes

Your notes

Your notes

Your notes